Not Just the Economy
The Public Value of Adult Learning

Edited by

Colin Flint and Chris Hughes

promoting adult learning

© 2008 National Institute of Adult Continuing Education
(England and Wales)

21 De Montfort Street
Leicester
LE1 7GE

Company registration no. 2603322
Charity registration no. 1002775

NIACE has a broad remit to promote lifelong learning opportunities for adults.
NIACE works to develop increased participation in education and training,
particularly for those who do not have easy access because of class, gender,
age, race, language and culture, learning difficulties or disabilities,
or insufficient financial resources.

For a full catalogue of all NIACE's publications visit www.niace.org.uk/publications

Cataloguing in Publications Data
A CIP record for this title is available from the British Library

Cover design by Creative by Design
Designed and typeset by Refinecatch, Bungay
Printed and bound by Latimer Trend, Plymouth

ISBN 978 1 86201 332 2

Contents

Foreword

Ten years or more have passed since Jacques Delors and David Blunkett sketched out broad and generous horizons for lifelong learning. Their emphasis was on the fulfilled individual and the contented society: in Blunkett's memorable phrase, a nation 'at ease with itself'. Now our vision is more utilitarian, more defensive of economic prosperity in an increasingly hostile world.

Perhaps we should not be surprised. Lifelong learning is a political idea and the political *zeitgeist* has suffered blow after blow since the mid-1990s. We have had 9/11 and 7/7. We have had the disillusionments of the Iraq war and every machination around it – devastatingly summarised by Thomas Ricks* in the single word 'fiasco'. We look forward through economic storm clouds that we had once been assured, and may have even believed, had vanished for ever in some miraculous post-modern economics. It is our sourer selves who must create the lifelong learning of the next decade.

There has been no shortage of Cassandras in learning and skills. Andrew Foster told further education firmly that its job was to create skills, jobs and wealth; stick to the knitting. Lord Leitch catalogued our every woe from ageing to low productivity to widespread ignorance of even the most basic communication skills. If all that was not enough, along came the certainty of global warming to tell us that even as we become more productive we raise the chances of cooking or drowning. Amid such a cacophony of exhortation and instruction that we are bound to be convinced that we are dammed if we do and damned if we don't, this book seeks to raise the gentle voice of reason.

The idea of public value can appear disconcertingly vague. We sort of know what it means but furrow our brows when working out how to get more of it. What it provides, however, is a means to weigh up the relative importance of differing responses to the clamour around us.

Lifelong learning has a future. In a country where people live longer, work longer, change activities more often and ebb and flow across the world needing new languages, adaptive strategies, it must have. The questions are the practical ones. How do we make it more popular? Where do we provide it conveniently? Who pays?

It is, in some ways, something of a relief that our government has set out its priorities and it is not unreasonable that they should cluster around wealth creation. We should not resent that. But neither should we accept that government priorities define the whole span of the horizon. We can choose. Employers will choose. Every learner will choose. And we will all choose according to our calculations of personal and public value.

Many people will see it as ironic that the mechanisms of lifelong learning have become greatly more secure and sophisticated in the past decade. It is a basic tenet of lifelong learning that formal learning, non-formal and informal learning should count equally for the purposes of formal qualification. Today, England is one of the few countries well on the way to having a national qualifications framework which can do this job and which matches the eight levels of the European Qualifications

* Thomas E Ricks, *Fiasco: the American military adventures in Iraq.* Penguin, 2006

Framework precisely. I have seen others anxious to achieve that. It is a basic tenet of lifelong learning that age should not disqualify access to appropriate study or certification. The various entitlements to at least basic qualifications now bundled in the Foundation Learning Tier and progress in lifting the upper age limits of programmes like apprenticeship, move us in that direction. It is a basic tenet of lifelong learning that it should come to the learner: at work, in the community, at home. We are well on the way to achieving that, thanks to broader definitions of public service which have been staked out steadily in the last ten years. It is a basic tenet of lifelong learning that higher education should not stand apart. Foundation degrees awarded by further education colleges and companies as well as the long-established and genuinely global excellence of the Open University are taking us there. Information technology and learning technologies are progressively making the timeworn demarcations meaningless.

Lifelong learning is coming and coming fast. How disappointing then, that a reduction of public subsidy should apparently decimate learning for personal fulfilment. Sad in itself, but raising the uncomfortable suspicion among NIACE members early in 2007 that, if learning was so price sensitive, it might be regarded as a branch of the entertainment industry by many in our society, rather than a cultural and human good beyond price. For many of us, that suspicion shook assumptions dearly held throughout a professional lifetime in learning. A year later, another drop of nearly 20 per cent in the number of adults taking part in state-subsidised learning and a fall in the number of people over 60 of over half justify Alan Tuckett's description; 'devastation'.

It is to perplexities of that kind that the papers in this book are addressed. They do what NIACE should do: present passionately held and well argued points of view. There are no easy or complete answers. The times and the issues are too complex. What these are, are ways into making hard choices with incomplete information about lifelong learning – something about which there is little consensus except that it is a necessity.

David Sherlock CBE
President of NIACE

David Sherlock

David is President of NIACE. He was formerly Chief Inspector of Adult Learning for England and chief executive of the Adult Learning Inspectorate (ALI). He is a fellow of the City and Guilds of London and a board member of the Qualifications and Curriculum Authority. He has a research degree from the University of Nottingham. In addition to 14 years in inspection David had 18 years' experience as vice-principal and principal of several colleges. He is a member of the Institute of Directors and a fellow of the Royal Society of Arts.

David is a director of Beyond Standards Limited, a consultancy specialising in quality and business improvement in education and training. The company has a strong client list in the UK and overseas. With his business partner, Nicky Perry, he has written *Quality Improvement in Adult Vocational Education and Training* for Kogan Page, to be published April 2008. He was awarded the CBE for services to lifelong learning in 2006.

Abbreviations and Acronyms

APL   accreditation of prior learning
CBI   Confederation of British Industry
CEL   Centre for Excellence in Leadership
DfEE   Department for Education and Employment
DfES   Department for Education and Skills
DIUS   Department for Innovation, Universities and Skills
DTI   Department of Trade and Industry
DWP   Department for Work and Pensions
ESOL   English for Speakers of Other Languages
FE   Further Education
FEFC   Further Education Funding Council
FLT   Foundation Learning Tier
Foster   The Foster Review of FE (2005)
GDP   Gross Domestic Product
HE   Higher Education
HMSO   Her Majesty's Stationery Office
IAG   Information Advice and Guidance
ICT   Information Communications Technology
IER   Institute for Employment Research
ILA   Individual Learning Accounts
ILEA   Inner London Education Authority
IPPR   Institute for Public Policy Research
LEAFEA   Local Education Authorities Forum for the education of adults
LCC   London County Council
LGA   Local Government Association
LMI   Labour Market Intelligence
LSDA   Learning and Skills Development Agency
LSC   Learning and Skills Council
LSN   Learning and Skills Network
Leitch   The Leitch Review of Skills 2007
NESS   National Employer Skills Survey
NIACE   National Institute for Adult Continuing Education
NPM   New Public Management
NOCN   National Open College Network
NRDC   National Research Development Council
NTO   National Training Organisation
NVQ   National Vocational Qualification
OECD   Organisation for European Cooperation and Development
PISA   Programme for International Student Assessment
QCA   Qualifications and Curriculum Authority
QCF   Qualifications and Credit Framework
QIA   Quality Improvement Agency
SBS   Small Business service
SME   Small and Medium Enterprises
SSC   Sector Skills Council
SSDA   Sector Skills Development Agency
TEC   Training and Enterprise Council
WEA   Workers' Educational Association

CHAPTER 1

Skills in a global economy

CHRIS HUMPHRIES

Summary

The skills challenges facing the UK are complex and significant, and becoming increasingly well understood. What is certain is that a policy of 'more of the same', or even of slow evolutionary improvements, will simply not produce the radical change in skills and productivity that is essential for the UK's continuing economic competitiveness and for ensuring a more inclusive society for all citizens.

The time is right for another step change in policy and strategy, building on recent success, but with renewed innovation, energy, focus and commitment. It is hoped that the ten proposals presented below might contribute to making that step change a substantial and successful one.

Introduction

Over the last ten years, workforce skills have grown in increasing importance on government agendas around the world as the realities of global competition have become clearer. The unusual and simultaneous threats and opportunities posed by new technologies, the progressive liberalisation of international trade, and the increasing mobility of capital and labour, require each nation to be clear on where its strengths and unique opportunities for economic growth and security lie.

Thomas Friedman, in his exciting and disturbing 2005 book *The World is Flat*, describes his story as 'a tale of technology and geoeconomics that is fundamentally reshaping our lives – much, much more quickly than many people realize.'[1] We are faced with significant opportunities for levelling the economic playing field for the world's nations, as well as challenges for both developing and developed countries to find their place in a world in which the rules are rapidly changing.

A key risk for the planet is that of exclusion. We are already seeing the political consequences of a growing gap between national 'haves' and 'have nots', and must strive to ensure that all nations are assisted to benefit – i.e. that

---

Why does this matter?

"A competitive society is one which achieves a dynamic equilibrium between wealth creation and social cohesion"

Prof. Stephane Garelli, Editor, World Competitiveness Handbook, 1995

- Economic and organisational competitiveness
- Individual engagement and potential
- Equity and social cohesion

Figure 1.1 Why does this matter?

the economic playing field really does begin to level. An equivalent risk exists at the national level, and governments must ensure that the benefits of a strong economy are able to be accessed by the population as a whole, and that the divide between the richer and poorer citizens narrows, rather than continuing to widen as seems to be happening currently in the UK. The recent social troubles in France and across much of Europe are other signs that this risk is very real.

It is essential that national governments respond to these challenges in a way that helps to build what Professor Stephane Garelli described in the 1995 World Competitiveness Handbook as a 'competitive society' – 'one which achieves a dynamic equilibrium between wealth creation and social cohesion.'

For any developed nation, economic development and social cohesion are two sides of the same coin. They are necessarily intertwined, as a strong economy is essential to create the opportunities needed to help each individual achieve their full potential, and to support those whose opportunities for personal growth and success may be limited by personal or social circumstance.

The Prime Minister said recently 'the best form of social inclusion is a job'. An acid test for any national strategy for a sound economic future is the extent to which it truly creates this equilibrium between economic competitiveness and social inclusion.

Omnipresent change

The drivers of economic change are many and interact in complex ways, with countries at different starting points, and with varying natural, economic and social strengths and weaknesses.

Each nation must understand its own position on the spectrum of change relating to each of the drivers. Whilst technology may be ubiquitous, it impacts

---

Drivers of industry and occupational change

- Technological change = making the improbable possible
- Political change = market and labour mobility
- Generational change = less conformist, more individualist
- Business change = companies like 'tents, not pyramids'*
- Older workers + birth rate decline = 'inverted workplace'
- Life expectancy = impact on health costs and pensions
- Online education = making skills more accessible

*Acknowledgement to Peter Drucker, *Management Challenges for the 21st Century*, 2003

Figure 1.2 Drivers of industry and occupational change
Source: worldtocom.comfutures network, 2004

on different societies in different ways. Countries like China are adopting cellular telephony on a grand scale, eased by the fact that they do not have an existing wired infrastructure holding them back. The impact of demographic change is most profound in Europe (plus Japan) with China preparing itself for a major "agequake" over the coming decade. Birth rates are beginning to decline in Africa and the Indian sub-continent, but their populations will still continue to grow for many years yet.

I will look at a number of these 'drivers of change' in more detail later. The important message is that the pace of change in different nations is extremely varied, as is their position in the change cycle. This is actually a helpful situation which could assist each nation in finding a unique equilibrium matched to their needs.

But change is not restricted to the political, technological and social arenas. Work and occupations themselves are changing, as technology fundamentally alters business processes, manufacturing becomes commoditised, innovation increases, product lifecycles shorten, and the skills required for work increase both in level and complexity.

For the developed world, ignoring these changes is not an option. The UK cannot expect to compete with China or India, or indeed even Eastern Europe, as just another low skill, low valued added player. We must up our game, using advanced knowledge and innovation to add value, and escalate rapidly to a high skill, high added value economy.

Whilst the UK's reputation *for* invention may be justifiably high, our track record *in* innovation ('the *successful exploitation* of new ideas')[2] and productivity is not. The UK has consistently underperformed too many of our key competitors on productivity and innovation since the 1960s.

Global changes in occupations

- Increasing skills levels – 80 per cent Level 3 by 2010 (UK)
- Fuzzy skill sets – generic job titles
- Team working, with shallower hierarchies and de-layering
- Multi-skilling and cross-skilling
- More staff customer facing with authority to act
- Flexible working practices – increasing variety
- 'Leadership and management' as key employability skills

Figure 1.3 Global changes in occupations

Figure 1.4 confirms the latest position through the OECD's 2004 productivity data. Whilst that data does show that we have closed the gap with the US and other key competitors a little over the last two years, with only Finland improving faster, the gap is still daunting and will take ten years or more to close completely if we sustain the current rate of improvement.

The underlying causes of this gap are complex, with the major contributor being 50 years of systematic under-investment in UK industry. Short-termism,

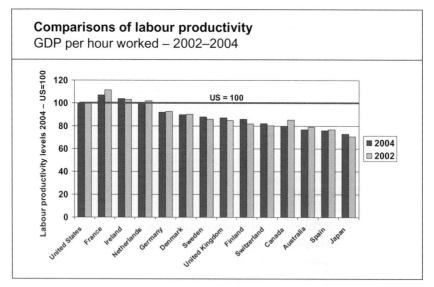

Figure 1.4 Comparisons of labour productivity
Source: OECD, International Comparisons of Labour Productivity Levels–Estimates for 2004, July 2005

driven by the boom and bust economic cycles of successive governments of both colours over that period, has left a legacy of relatively poor infrastructure and facilities that has bedevilled British manufacturing. The last ten years of economic stability has improved the situation markedly, but it will be some decades before we can fully compensate for that damage.

Skills matter

Skills, too, are a known and significant contributor to productivity. Importantly, they have the added advantages of being more amenable to solution in the medium term, than investment, and contribute directly to social inclusion. But how significant a contribution can skills really make to improving productivity? And is the evidence strong enough to convince employers and national governments of the benefits?

In manufacturing, the evidence is strong. This study, discussed in HM Treasury's Pre-Budget Report in 2002, sets it out clearly. In a carefully controlled study, researchers found that doubling the ratio of high skilled to low skilled staff in UK manufacturing plants actually moved them from the lowest quartile in productivity to the highest quartile – from trailing edge to leading edge through one investment. If that investment was in a capital asset producing a similar effect, every manufacturing company would be lining up to buy one!

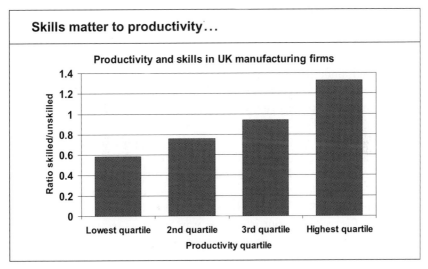

Figure 1.5 Skills and productivity in manufacturing
Source: Barnes and Haskel, 2000, in *Developing Workforce Skills*, HM Treasury, 2002

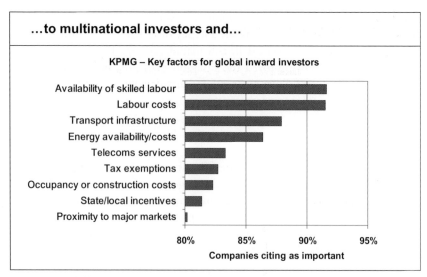

...to multinational investors and...

KPMG – Key factors for global inward investors

Figure 1.6 Skills and inward investment
Source: KPMG Competitive Alternatives Report, 2002

But the evidence is stronger, and a second tranche comes from those multinational corporates who make most of the major inward investments around the world. KPMG occasionally produce their Competitive Alternatives Report, surveying all the significant inward investors on what factors most inform decisions on location.

The message in their 2002 report was quite clear, with availability of skilled labour at the top of the list. International investment follows skills, and such investors know what makes the biggest difference to their success.

Less well understood is the impact that investment in skills has on shareholder return – that critical influencer of corporate behaviour. Research by Bassi Investments, reported in the Milken Institute Review in 2004 (see Figure 1.7), tracked the performance of a share portfolio of companies with high investments in training over five years, against the "Standard and Poor 500" average (a US equivalent of the FTSE 500).

The findings were clear: a portfolio of US firms that made the largest investments in employee skills produced the larger return (16.3 per cent p.a.) compared to the average return (10.7 per cent) for the Standard and Poor 500 index over five years. To put it another way, investors receive a 52 per cent higher return over five years from shares in companies that make high investments in training than from tracking the index. In a fully informed market, with open reporting of corporate investment in quality training, the shareholder imperative for training would be very high.

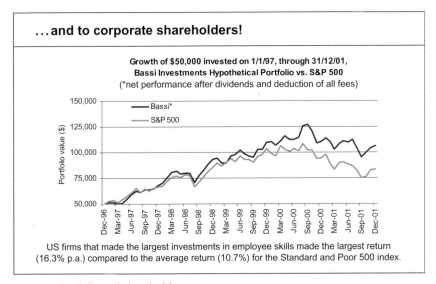

...and to corporate shareholders!

Growth of $50,000 invested on 1/1/97, through 31/12/01,
Bassi Investments Hypothetical Portfolio vs. S&P 500
(*net performance after dividends and deduction of all fees)

US firms that made the largest investments in employee skills made the largest return (16.3% p.a.) compared to the average return (10.7%) for the Standard and Poor 500 index.

Figure 1.7 Skills and shareholder return
Source: Bassi and McMurrer, "Are Skills Costs or Assets?" Milken Institute Review, Q3, 2004

The ageing workforce – a European problem

It is not only industries and nations that are changing – the workforce itself is going through a period of unprecedented evolution. This may sound an extreme claim, but the nature of demographic change affecting the UK workforce – indeed, workforces across the whole of Europe – really does represent what author Paul Wallace called an 'agequake'.[3]

Figures 1.8a and 1.8b show the scale of change in the demographics of the workforce. The traditional workforce shape of 1995 – with progressively less workers in each five-year higher age range – effectively inverts to the shape shown below, with less young workers, and older workers forming the largest segment of employment, by 2020.

There are two primary underlying causes of this change. The UK birth rate fell dramatically during the 1990s, from 2.4 live births per woman lifetime in the census of 1991 to 1.6 in the 2001 census. For the first time, the UK birth rate fell below the so-called 'replacement rate' of 2.1 live births per woman lifetime, and it fell dramatically. The major workplace impact of this will begin to be felt from 2010 onwards, when the number of young people reaching working age (15–24 years old) will begin to fall by 60,000 every year from 2010 to 2020, i.e. the number of 15- to 24-year-olds in the UK in 2020 will be 600,000 less than in 2010.

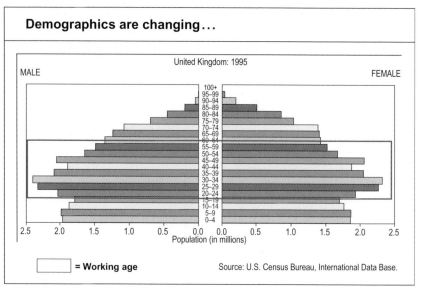

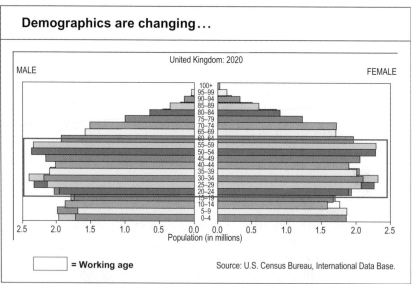

Figures 1.8a and 1.8b The ageing workforce – 1995 versus 2020

The second cause is more widely understood, and is the extraordinary increase in longevity that has resulted from improved efficacy of modern medical care. Not only does this mean that people can physically work longer, but pension coverage and boredom means that some adults are now actively seeking opportunities to work beyond traditional retirement age. Yet over the last 30 years, whilst these pressures have been increasing, the actually working life of the average UK worker has been shrinking, squeezed at both ends, by young people staying longer in education, and the growth in early retirement.

This presents a number of serious challenges for employers in terms of workforce development:

- the competition between industries and employers to attract young people to their occupations and businesses will become fiercer, as there will simply not be enough young recruits to go round;
- employers will have to begin to target older workers and the non-employed to support forecast employment growth over the next 15 years;
- older workers seeking to extend their careers or enter new ones will have to engage in yet more learning if their skills are to continue to be relevant over a working lifetime of perhaps 50 years rather than 35 to 40;
- employers are going to have to develop new forms of opportunity and incentives to attract and retain young people in a workforce which, for the first time in modern industrial history will be 'top-heavy' with older workers.

Demographic change also represents a particular challenge for Europe. An analysis of the worlds '20 oldest countries' (in terms of the proportion of the population over 65) shows that 19 of the top 20 are in Europe, with the one honourable exception being Japan.

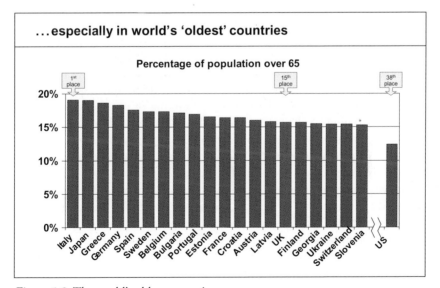

Figure 1.9 The world's oldest countries
Source: U.S. Census Bureau, International Data Base (New data April 2005)

China is quite likely to enter this club over the next 15 years, as their 'one child per family policy' has caused their birth rate to drop below the replacement rate (to around 1.7) for each of the last ten years. Even birth rates in the Indian sub-continent and Africa are beginning to fall sharply, though they are some decades away yet from European levels. Intriguingly, America shows no sign yet of any significant fall in birth rate, and is forecast to avoid most of these demographic challenges until 2025 onwards.

Industry and occupational change

Much of the impact of technological innovation over the last 20 years has been to change fundamentally the balance of industry and occupations that make up the economic landscape in developed countries.

Whilst that change has undoubtedly been very significant, the hype has often outweighed the reality. Over that extended period, media headlines have prematurely announced the death of engineering and manufacturing, the end of low skilled jobs, the continuing decline of construction employment, the conversion of the UK to a wholly service economy, or a wholly knowledge- (as distinct from skills-) based economy.

In almost every case, these claims have misunderstood and misrepresented the available evidence, and significantly influenced career decisions by young people in unhelpful and inappropriate ways.

Let me first look at industry change (Figure 1.10).

The broad trends shown here are consistent with the general thrust of media messages – it is the scale of change, and the slope of the trend lines that have been greatly exaggerated. Direct employment in engineering and manufacturing has indeed declined over the period, though much of the change has resulted from the outsourcing of non-manufacturing functions (logistics, marketing, IT, etc.) as well as from the off-shoring of commoditised manufacturing operations. Still over 3 million jobs are offered within the sector, and skill shortages (as we will see below) are serious.

Construction employment, far from declining as media hype would have it, has actually stayed broadly constant for the last 20 years.

Growth has been strongest in business services, followed closely by non-marketed (primarily public) services, though as we will see below, growth in sectors (or occupations) does not necessarily imply skills shortages. In fact, the position is often the contrary.

Figure 1.11 shows the patterns of actual and forecast change in occupations over the 30 years from 1982–2012, from research published by the Institute for Employment Research and DfES in 2004.

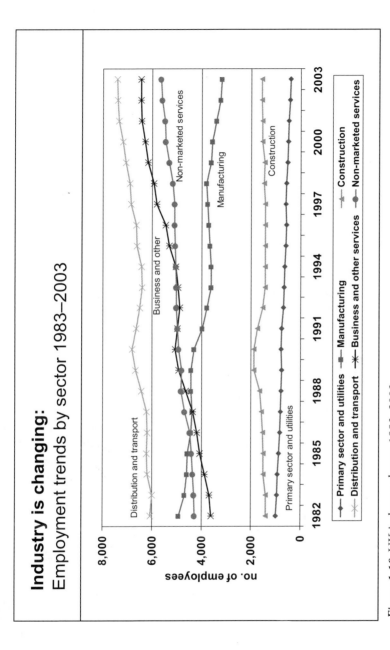

Figure 1.10 UK industry change 1983–2003
Source: IER estimates, drawn from LSC, Skills in England 2004, July 2005, Vol. 2, p. 29

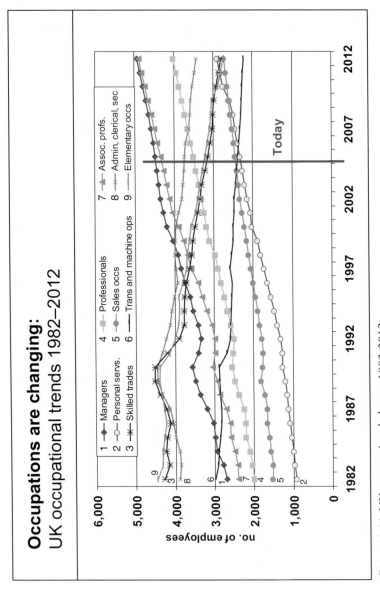

Figure 1.11 UK occupational change 1982-2012

Source: DfES, Working Futures, National Report 2003–04, IER, 2004

It highlights that, whilst employment in occupations such as traditional crafts and trades and low-skilled work has been declining, alongside growth in professional, associate professional and service occupations, the idea that the former are disappearing to be replaced by the latter is grossly exaggerated. The balance of occupations is undoubtedly changing over time, but there will be both a need for, and significant opportunities in, the widest spectrum of occupations for many years to come.

This need is reinforced further when the future decade's forecast data is examined in more detail. There are two distinct elements to future occupational requirements. The most publicised relates to the net increase or decrease in the total requirement for each occupation – the difference between the total number of, say skilled trades, required in 2002, and the number that will be required in 2012 (the 'new growth/decline' data in Figure 1.12). But of course many of the occupants of the jobs that will exist at both ends of the decade, retire, change careers, die or emigrate, and those jobs also form part of the future recruitment requirements – what is called 'replacement demand'. The black lines in Figure 1.12 show the total 'overall demand' which results from the sum of 'replacement' and 'new' demand.

The UK will need to replace or fill 2.5 million associate professional and technical jobs in the decade from 2002–2012 – it will also need 800,000 skilled craftsmen and women. Whether that need becomes a problem or not depends, of course, not only on the demand, but also on the supply of available

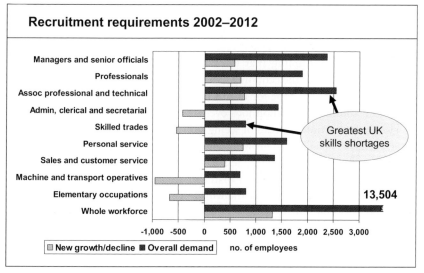

Figure 1.12 UK occupational requirements 2002–2012
Source: DfES, Working Futures, National Report 2003–04, IER, 2004

skilled labour. I'll look at where the key skills shortages are in more detail below, and what that evidence will show is that the greatest UK skills shortages are currently being experienced in the occupational areas where there is both the most, and (almost) the least, overall demand.

The well documented problem in skilled trades results not from overwhelming future demand, but from the combination of an ageing workforce (in some sectors and occupations, 50 per cent or more of the existing workforce are due to retire in the next ten years), and the serious decline in the number of enrolments by young people in vocational and technical careers since the early 1990s.

There is one further feature of Figure 1.12 that needs to be examined against the demographic changes presented earlier – the figure relating to the total number of new jobs forecast to enter the economy. The IER forecasts suggest that 1.35 million new jobs will enter the economy between 2002 and 2012. However, because of the 1990s birth rate decline, the number of young people (15–24 years old) entering the workforce over that period will only grow by 500,000.

There is an obvious question that needs asking here – by whom will the other 850,000 new jobs be filled? Immigration will be part of the solution, but only part, and the rest can only come from yet another increase in the level of employment amongst adults. Simply put, those jobs will have to be filled by a combination of more currently employed adults working longer, and more of those who are currently registered unemployed or non-employed choosing to enter the workforce.

But the real problem is waiting round the corner in the next decade. Because, as highlighted earlier on page 4, from 2010 to 2020, the number of young people entering the labour market doesn't rise at all, it falls by 600,000 over the decade. Assuming that the Chancellor's aspiration (and ours, if we have any sense) is that the economy will continue to grow over that next decade by at least the rate we hope for in this decade, the predictions suggest that we will create another 1.5 million jobs over the ten years from 2010 to 2020.

However, this time, instead of seeing over a third of those new jobs being at least partially filled by a growing number of young people entering the workforce, there will be 600,000 less young people. Unless very large numbers of adults work significantly longer than they do today, the total number of new adults who would need to enter the workforce to achieve a similar growth rate would be 1.5 million (new jobs) + 600,000 (to make up for the missing young people) i.e. 2.1 million. This is a seriously challenging target, which can only be met through a combination of managed immigration, most adults working longer, a huge increase in the number of currently unemployed or non-employed adults entering the labour force – all of whom must have the skills appropriate for jobs in the 2010–20 decade.

To summarise so far:

- the UK (and most other European nations) are entering an era of extreme competition from the developing and 'flattening' world;
- the developing world's young population is still increasing rapidly, as is the quality of their education systems (see below) so they can build their economies on increasing numbers of dynamic and better educated young people;
- in order to compete, developed countries like the UK will have to ensure they are operating high skill, high value added economies;
- and we will have to develop such economies by building in significant part on the back of the skills already held by the existing workforce, and substantial numbers of the currently unemployed and non-employed.

It is clearly essential that the UK offers a high quality school education system that successfully maximises the potential of every young person in our population (see below), but that will only be a necessary, not a sufficient condition for remaining economically competitive with tomorrow's fast-moving giants like China, India, and Brazil.

The challenge of adult skills

Our dependence on the skills of those adults already in the workforce is increasing rapidly. So, a rather important question for the UK and other 'ageing' developed countries is – how good are the skills of our working age adult population? It is to that question I now turn.

The short answer to the question is clearly demonstrated by Figure 1.13 – and is not good! The latest (2005) OECD data shows that the level of attainment (in terms of highest qualification held) of adults of working age in the UK falls into the lower half of OECD countries.

How, as a developed country, with a sound reputation for its education system, have we got into this state? The simple reason appears to lie in the fact that our school education system serves one half of the population – those with strong academic leanings – extremely well, but singularly fails the other half. Only 51 per cent of our young people actually achieve the formal measure of five GCSEs at grades A*–C (the benchmark for Level 2 in the English system), and the milestone of 50 per cent of 16-year-olds gaining Level 2 was only reached in the twenty-first century.

The UK has one of the lowest levels of participation in learning by 17-year-olds of any nation in the OECD. Young people who achieve five GCSEs at grades A*–C by age 16 continue studying, but those who don't achieve that learning outcome disengage significantly.

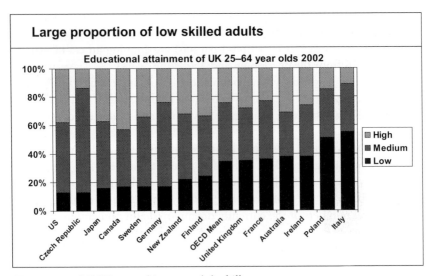

Figure 1.13 OECD – working age adult skills
Source: OECD, Education at a Glance, 2005, Table A1.1a

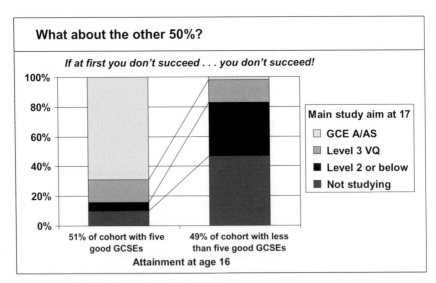

Figure 1.14 What about the other 50%?
Source: DfES Corporate Strategy, 2004; Main study aim of 17-year-olds by Year 11 attainment

Figure 1.15 UK workforce skills 2004

Source: DfEE/DfES, Labour Force Survey, 1989–2004, latest data quoted in LSC, Skills in England 2004, IER 2005

This is not a recent phenomenon. It is instead a fundamental feature of our foundation learning system that has shaped the experience of every age group since the 1944 Education Act (and to be frank, long before that).

Figure 1.15 confirms that we have been making some progress in raising skill levels over the last 15 years, but also highlights how big the gap between demand and supply still remains.

The projections presented earlier by the Institute for Employment Research (Figures 1.11 and 1.12), as well as forecasts by business bodies like the Confederation of British Industry, suggest that up to 75 per cent of 2012 jobs are likely to require skills to at least Level 3, but only 50 per cent of the 2004 workforce skills had attained that level in 2004. That suggests a requirement to raise skill levels for 25 per cent of the workforce, or 7 million people, from Level 2 or lower to Level 3 within the next seven years.

Rising skill demands also mean that no more than 10–15 per cent of 2012 jobs are likely to require low or unskilled workers, and yet in 2004, that figure still stands at 30 per cent. Again, a simple calculation suggests a requirement to raise another 4.5 million people from low or no skills to Level 2 over the same period.

This is a seriously challenging agenda, and indeed will require far higher participation, and success levels than current policy and funding is targeted to produce. With an estimated 20 per cent of the adult population still lacking the levels of literacy and numeracy necessary to successfully participate in learning, it will also require a continuing priority focus on adult basic skills.

More adults working longer

We've seen earlier that the youth cohort decline from 2010–2020 will require yet more engagement of the adult population in employment, with the IER estimating that the employment levels for men and women of working age will need to approach 80 per cent in order to meet forecast employment growth.

Undoubtedly, the pensions crisis will help address some of this growth by persuading people to work longer, and the government is already examining ideas for raising retirement age and other incentives/sanctions to persuade older employees to work longer. But 2.1 million people is a lot of new entrants to the adult workforce in a decade (2010–2020) – particularly where most of them are to be drawn from the unemployed and non-employed.

And the skills challenge will be even greater than we have experienced so far. Figure 1.16 confirms fears that many have often expressed – that the proportion of the non-employed (those adults not in work who are not registered with Job Centre Plus) with no qualifications at all is much higher than amongst the employed, or even the registered unemployed. The task of developing higher skills amongst the non-employed is going to be much tougher than the work currently underway with Employer Training Pilots, and the new National Employer Training Programme, in England.

The observant reader will of course respond, 'But surely Figure 1.15 shows that we have been making consistent progress on adult skills since 1989?', and

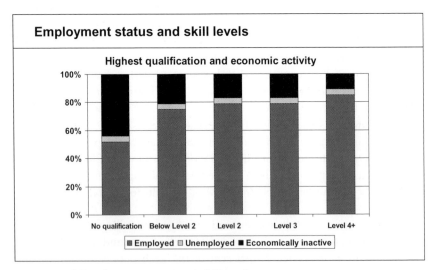

Figure 1.16 Employment status and skill levels
Source: Labour Force Survey, 2003

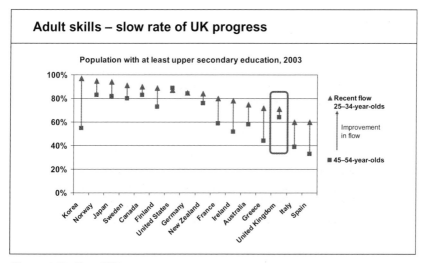

Figure 1.17 Slow UK progress
Source: OECD, Education at a Glance 2005, page 31

of course it does. What is doesn't indicate is whether that improvement is happening fast enough, and what our competitors have been doing over the same period.

Once again, the OECD comparisons are both informative and very unreassuring.

The reality (Figure 1.17) is that the UK has been in the bottom half of the OECD league table on adult skills for the last 20 years. Our rate of improvement over that period has been the slowest of all those bottom-half nations.

(And it may be slowing further – Figure 1.21 below references DfES research that shows almost no improvement has occurred in the five years from 1998 to 2003). Whilst we've been improving slowly, our competitors have been accelerating past us, and our relative position has worsened considerably.

Most of the improvement in the skills of the working age population over the last 20 years has resulted from the 'flow' of increasing skill levels of young people entering the labour market, not from improvements in the skills of the 'stock' of the existing labour force. And although the flow is improving slowly, it is doing so from a low starting point. The clear message from the OECD data is that the 'flow' isn't improving fast enough to solve the UK's 'stock' problem; and the message from the demographic data is that the flow will be decreasing in the coming decade, making the stock issue – the need to upskill the existing working age population – even more essential.

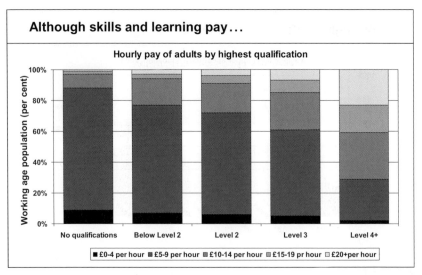

Figure 1.18 Skills and learning pay
Source: *Skills in the Global Economy,* HM Treasury, 2005, p. 11, derived from Labour Force Survey, Winter 2003

Engaging adults in learning

It's extremely difficult to raise skill levels amongst adults of working age without their willing and active participation, and many need as much convincing that learning is 'worth it', as employers need convincing that skills are assets worthy of investment, not just costs.

Learning does pay! The return to adults participating in formal learning in terms of hourly pay (Figure 1.18) is significant and progressive, particularly as skill levels rise above the effective 'entry level' for employment – Level 2. For low skilled adults, the premium for learning to Level 2 is still significant though lower, as is the return on the basic skills of literacy and numeracy.

The pay premium from learning is also not limited to the young, a concern that has been expressed by older workers when encouraged to participate in upskilling programmes. The Department for Education and Skills published research in 2003[4] that showed that the return on learning for adults not only continues with age, but in many cases, the wage premium actually increases for older workers (Figure 1.19).

Which leads us to the great anomaly, never really satisfactorily explained other than in terms of UK cultural attitudes, as to why, when the benefits of skills to business productivity and to individual earnings are clear, investment in skills is inversely proportional to need.

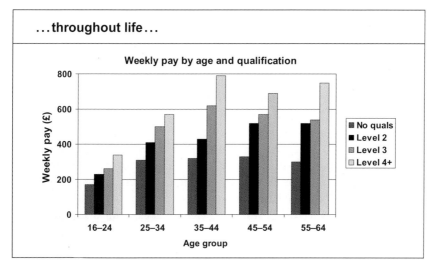

Figure 1.19 Skills and learning pay throughout life
Source: *Education and Skills: The Economic Benefits,* DfES, 2003, p. 17

The return to productivity from upskilling low skilled staff is high, yet employers consistently prioritise their spending on training to those with the highest level of skills, not the lowest. The return to earnings for workers of all levels is high, but those who we most need to raise their skills are the group least likely to voluntarily participate (Figure 1.20).

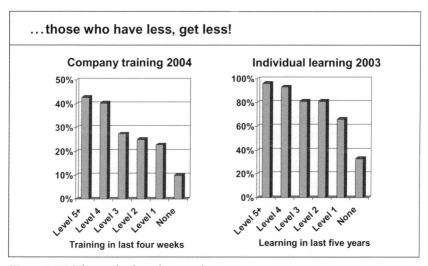

Figure 1.20 Those who have less, get less
Source: LSC, *Skills in England 2004,* IER 2005; *Education and Skills: The Economic Benefits,* DfES, 2003, p. 17

In other words, the current provision of training for adults, by and large, increases the gap between the learning rich and learning poor – and thus the earnings rich and earnings poor – rather than decreases it. If anything, the slope of the graph of company training against prior skills levels has actually worsened over the last ten years, with more, rather than less investment in personal development, drifting towards the already highly educated.

Any set of policies designed to significantly increase adult participation in work related learning and skills must seek to overcome the set of attitudes, beliefs and cultural mores amongst individuals and employers that fundamentally perceive access to learning as an elitist right that only brings benefits to the already privileged. Information, understanding, the positive promotion of the benefits, advice and guidance for adults, and the removal of barriers to access, perceived or real, will be essential elements of any successful adult engagement strategy.

What and where are the gaps?

Understanding the scale of the problem is only half the challenge, evidence is also needed on the nature of the skills gaps we face, and numerous studies are available to help clarify the situation. One of the most interesting, because it has now been conducted three times over an eight-year period, is the DfES Skills Audit.

Conducted in 1996, and published in full in 1997, the initial Skills Audit represented the first systematic attempt to benchmark UK skill levels against our major global competitors. Examining both government data, and evidence from multinational companies operating in all studied countries, publishing the Skills Audit was a brave government decision to highlight a significant UK deficit, particularly at what is called the intermediate level (particularly Levels 3 and 4 – skilled craft workers and associate professionals).

A further data update was conducted in 1998 and published in 1999, and the DfES then commissioned the original authors in 2003 to review comparisons between the UK, France, Germany, Singapore and the US (Figure 1.21).

On training to Level 2, the report summary was succinct: "The UK has the lowest proportion of the active population with a Level 2 or higher qualification of all the countries compared". On training to Level 3, the report appeared to offer some good news, but with a sting in the tail.

Between 1994 and 2003, the UK had achieved the fastest growth of all five nations in the proportion of 21-year-olds attaining either a Level 2 or Level 3 qualification. Sadly, two other findings somewhat soured the good news. The trend in the UK has been to treat the period for post-compulsory 'foundation learning' for young people as encompassing the ages 16–21. Our funding

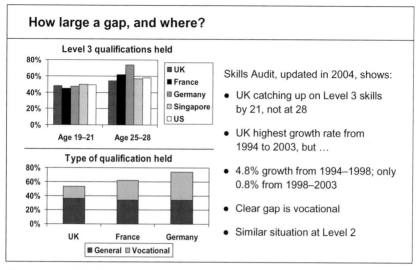

Figure 1.21 What's the gap?
Source: DfES Research Report RR548, International Comparisons of Qualifications Held: Skills Audit Update, 2004

regimes prioritise learning to 19, increasing fees above that age, and our targets do likewise.

What the research highlighted was that in Europe, particularly, but also in Singapore and the US to a lesser extent, young people continue to engage in learning up to the age of 25. As a result, the gap between the UK and these key competitors widens back to the level it was in the original 1997 Skills Audit when we compare skill levels at age 25–28.

Of more concern was the evidence identified when all three studies were compared. Almost all the improvement in the skills of 19–21-year-olds, at both levels, had taken place between 1994 and 1998. From 1998 to 2003, the rate of improvement declined dramatically, and at Level 2, was almost negligible. Either what we had been doing right stopped working, or, more likely, those competitor countries have upped their game still further in recent years, and we must now do the same.

The employers' perspective

The evidence from the three Skills Audits provides a useful overview of skills levels and generic weaknesses across the breadth of sectors and occupations, but does not provide sufficient detail to help identify and respond to specific skill shortage priorities. For that, we need to turn to data directly from employers.

The National Employer Skills Survey (NESS) was first created by the Skills Task Force (1998–2000) as a response to its own criticism of the validity and comparability of available data on employer views on skills, whether collected by government or business lobby groups.

NESS is the most comprehensive survey of its kind, involving over 27,000 interviews with employers of different sizes across different sectors and localities in England, and is now conducted annually by the Learning and Skills Council. The most recent data comes from the survey conducted in 2004.

As previously highlighted in Figure 1.12, until 2003, the two largest areas of skills shortages were in skilled trades and associate professional and technical occupations. The 2004 data shows skills shortages in personal service occupations on the increase. The majority of skills for these groups of occupations lie at Levels 3 and 4. Machine and transport operatives (primarily Level 2) lie a close fourth, whilst shortages in professional and managerial occupations (primarily graduate level) have fallen to negligible levels, mostly the normal frictional gaps caused by recruitment timescales for senior positions.

The messages from this survey have not really changed significantly since the first survey published in 2000. As confirmed by the Skills Audit data, the UK's largest skill shortages – and future challenges – continue to lie at the intermediate levels in traditionally vocational occupations.

Employers are not just asked in the survey for information on the occupations in which they are experiencing skills shortages, they are also questioned to identify the types of skills they find difficult to recruit.

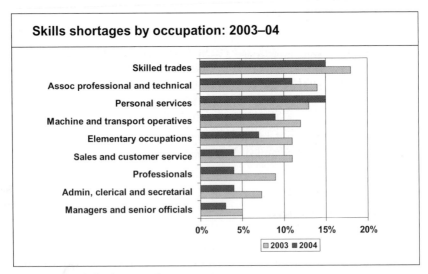

Skills shortages by occupation: 2003–04

Figure 1.22 Skills shortages by occupation
Source: LSC National Employer Skills Survey 2003 and 2004, IER

The last ten years has seen much debate over the balance in employers' requirements between technically specific occupational skills, and the generic employability skills like communication, numeracy, customer service, etc. "Employers don't want technical skills, all they need is recruits with the generic skills, and they will do the rest" has been a mantra often repeated, but little evidenced.

Every National Employer Skills Survey since the first has carried a very clear message: generic skills are important, but the biggest cause of skills shortages are specific technical occupational skills (Figure 1.23). Employability skills are necessary, but not sufficient, for employer competitiveness.

The final piece of the skills shortage jigsaw is the question of 'where'. We know the broad occupational priorities, but which sectors have the greatest challenges, and what can that tell us about our future strategy.

The 2004 NESS disaggregated its research to the constituent sub-sectors of the 25 new Sector Skills Councils in order to help inform and shape their priorities and future plans (Figure 1.24).

Again, the findings are consistent with earlier years, and reinforce the point made above in relation to Figure 1.12 – skills shortages result as often from lack of supply as they do from growth in demand. The top six sectors experiencing skills shortages are all sectors where data on industry change (Figure 1.10) shows that employment in the sector is declining slowly, not growing. Yet the combination of the data shown in Figures 1.11 and 1.12, with this skills shortage

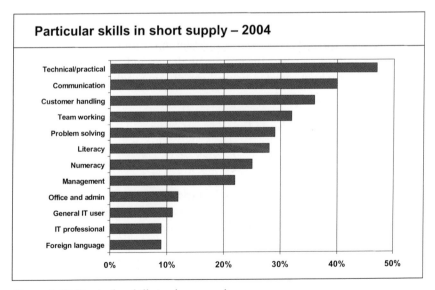

Figure 1.23 Particular skills in short supply
Source: LSC National Employer Skills Survey 2004, IFF

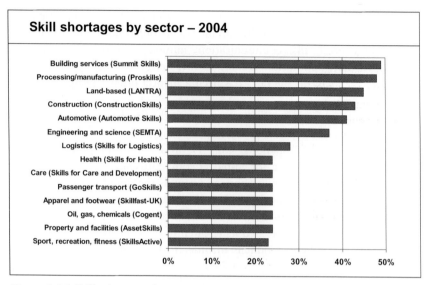

Figure 1.24 Skills shortages by sector
Source: LSC National Employer Skills Survey 2004, IFF

data, makes it clear that there will be productive employment opportunities for many years in these sectors, that salaries will benefit positively from the impact of supply shortages, and that these areas are critical for the future economy of UK plc.

This highlights the importance of ensuring that the information reaching young people, their parents and adults on opportunities in sectors and occupations really does reflect the realities on the ground, and not the rumours of the college or school corridor, or the hype of some of the media.

Implications for the labour force

The evidence base described above is both complex and entangled, so what messages does it send to individuals, employers and governments? Let me take each of these in turn, starting with individuals.

The demographic trend across Europe is clear – there will be 600,000 less young people aged 15–24 entering the UK labour force between 2010 and 2020. Employment growth in our economy over that period – potentially as much as 2.1 million net additional people in the labour market – will have to be met from adults already of working age. Young people will be in a seller's market, and could potentially even command recruitment premiums, except

Implications for the labour force

- Youth cohort is declining – a global trend, esp. Europe
- Requirement for more skilled adult workers, working longer
- Key/generic/employability skills an increasing issue
- Demand to be informed by future employment opportunity
- Currency of knowledge and skills is shortening
- Need to up-skill or re-skill five to ten times in working life
- Earnings improve with learning

↳ **Individuals compete (globally) on attitude and skills**

Figure 1.25 Implications for the labour force

in those sectors or employers where adult recruitment programmes provide sufficient replacement.

Adults already in work may contribute to this need by working longer, as may immigration, but the significant growth is likely to come from current unemployed or non-employed adults entering or re-entering the labour force.

The skills required for virtually all jobs are rising over time, and the currency of existing skills shortens with technological and organisational change. Generic employability skills will be important for every adult in the workforce if they are to be able to enhance their skills throughout their working lives, but the right balance and supply of technical skills will be essential.

Estimates by researchers and futurists suggest that each of us will have to reskill or upskill ourselves between five and ten times during our lengthening working life, if we are to maximise our future employability. Both young people and mobile adults will therefore require access to reliable labour market information that properly identifies future employment opportunities, based upon sound data and projections, if they are to make informed choices and, as a nation, we are to minimise skills shortages.

Because the reality is, in today's highly mobile markets, industry and employment will follow skills, and individuals will end up competing for future work on the basis of their attitudes and willingness to adapt and learn, and the extent to which they keep their skills ahead of the game.

Implications for employers

Employers, too, will face continuing challenges around skills, as the pace of technological and business change increases relentlessly. As product and service lifecycles reduce, driven by global innovation and open markets, companies in the developed world will have to learn to be yet more agile and responsive, and seriously raise their game in terms of productivity and value-added.

Skill levels required for employment will, as ever, continue to rise, but even more rapidly than before, and yet the flow of new skills and capability through young recruits will become rarer. In such an environment, companies will need to invest more, and incentivise their workforce to participate, in upskilling or re-skilling at key stages of their working lives, or risk losing their competitive edge through reducing innovation and productivity.

Most employers in many sectors will have to attract older 'new' recruits to meet future growth opportunities and, at the same time, understand the implications of managing a workforce in which the traditional age profile will be inverted. Imagine the challenge of motivating young workers through incentives and new opportunities, when their career ladder is blocked by older workers needing to work longer.

New patterns of working will need to be supported for and available to older workers (all workers?), including more part-time working, 'downshifting' (into less demanding roles), flexible hours and work locations, and many others.

In the twenty-first century, companies in the developed world will have little choice but to compete on the basis of productivity, innovation, value-added and their responsiveness to the challenges of markets in which the advantages of low costs and mass labour have passed to others. Working smarter requires smarter people, and the responsibility for ensuring that happens will sit firmly in the corporate boardroom.

In reality, of course, the challenges for adults and employers are closely linked. Employers need the commitment and positive engagement of their workforce in learning and development; individual participation and achieve-

---

Implications for employers

- Pace of technological and business change increasing
- Firms raise their game in value-added and productivity
- Skill levels rising across almost all job roles
- Need to attract older recruits alongside young
- Need to support more flexibility/new patterns of work
- Need to regularly invest in upskilling an aging workforce
- Learn how to manage an 'inverted workforce'

  ↳ **Employers compete on value-added and responsiveness**

Figure 1.26 Implications for employers

ment in learning and skills development is significantly increased through active support by employers who both encourage and incentivise successful learning.

The success of the Employer Training Pilots in England has confirmed that the most effective strategies for reaching employees, and particularly those with lower skills levels not recently engaged in successful learning, involve working with and through employers. Some of the most successful programmes of all have involved effective working partnerships between employers and supportive trade unions, demonstrating the benefits to individual employees, and providing both the managerial and peer support to maximise motivation, commitment and success.

So where do employees work? The UK statistics on companies and employment tend to highlight the very large numbers of small firms in Britain. One of the most common statistics on firms is that 97 per cent of employers have less than 50 employees – the vast majority of employers in Britain are small and medium enterprises (SMEs).

Whilst certainly true, this statistic is highly misleading when the challenge that is being addressed is 'how can we reach employees to encourage them to increase their skills?'. The better question to ask is 'where do the vast majority of employees work?'. When asked in this way, the statistics present a far more accessible answer, as shown in Figures 1.28 and 1.29.

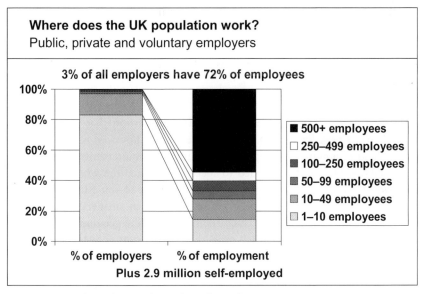

Figure 1.27 Where do people work – all employers?
Source: DTI/SBS, SME Statistics 2003, published December 2004 (not including 2.9 million self-employed)

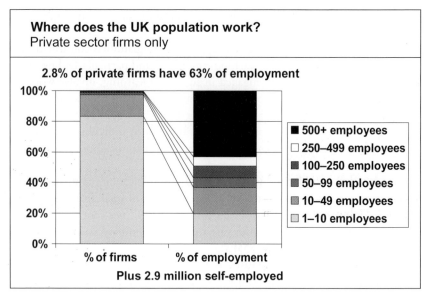

Figure 1.28 Where do people work – private sector?

The fact is, when all employers – private, public and voluntary – are taken into account, almost three-quarters of the workforce are employed by only 3 per cent of firms: all those employers with more than 50 employees. Designing and implementing programmes targeting the 37,000 organisations that employ these 17.6 million employees offers the fastest route to success for the majority of employees.

Even when the public and voluntary employers are taken out of the picture, 2.8 per cent of private employers still employ almost two-thirds of the workforce.

Such statements should not be taken as a suggestion that policy should ignore small firms, far from it. What it does imply, however, is that different policies and programmes, recognising the different requirements of large firms versus SMEs, may well be needed to successfully reach the whole workforce. The workforce in smaller employers is as important to our future as that in larger firms, and necessitates the effective targeting of smaller firms through separate initiatives that seek to reach them through the geographical, sectoral and supply chain clusters in which more than 80 per cent of SMEs are located.

Implications for nations

The overarching conclusions of this paper and presentation must be for nations. The evidence is clear – the success of national economies will depend

Implications for nations

- School systems must serve 100 per cent of youth
- Redress adult literacy and numeracy issues
- Ensure public education and training is employment led
- Prioritise/invest in vocational **and** academic education
- Grow proportion of workforce upskilling/reskilling
- Persuade/incentivise adults to (re-)engage in learning
- Address the 'who pays' problem – tripartite responsibility

  ↳ **Nations compete on their education system**

Figure 1.29 Implications for nations

on the productivity and competitiveness of their firms, and this in turn will be advanced or retarded by the skills of their people.

So nations will fundamentally continue to compete on the strengths and weaknesses of their education systems. In a world undergoing such demographic change, this must be an education system that ensures not only that their youth achieve a sound foundation of learning for work and adult life, but that their adult workforce has continuing opportunities to develop and adapt their skills in order to ensure individual opportunity and corporate success.

The intermediate level technical and vocational skills shortages experienced in the UK in recent years is a salutary reminder that we require a balanced education and training system that properly serves the economy's needs for both theoretical and practical skills. We cannot afford to squander the potential talent of any citizen, young or old, and have an obligation to ensure access to developmental learning at many points in people's lives.

Characteristics of a twenty-first century system

What then would be the characteristics of a twenty-first century education and training system that will ensure the UK can continue to compete effectively in the global market place? Let me set out my vision.

1. The school system would be adapted and re-designed to serve the needs of 100 per cent of young people – a system that fails half of the youth of England cannot be allowed to continue. The priority of the school system should be to provide coherent preparation for employability, future learning and adult life, offering a broad curriculum across general and vocational learning. It's purpose should not be to prepare young people for a job, but

Characteristics of a responsive twenty-first century education and training system

- Designed to serve **all** young people **and** adults
- Respond to/anticipate labour market change and demand
- Proper balance between academic and applied skills
- Standards and qualifications keeping pace with change
- Highly flexible by time, pace, place and mode of learning
- Close integration between institutions and the workplace
- Balanced investment from state, employer, individual according to need and benefit

Figure 1.30 Characteristics of a twenty-first century system

    to ensure that they can access the future learning and employment opportunities that will help them achieve their full potential. England should implement the full proposals of the Tomlinson Report.

2. The core purpose of our tertiary education system, and particularly the further education system, should be on providing learning and skills for employment. Sir Andrew Foster made this recommendation the centrepiece of his review of the further education system published on 15 November 2005, and I believe a similar expectation should apply to higher education. This is not an anti-research or anti-academic argument – research and academia are an important part of our labour market and contribute significantly to our economy – but it undoubtedly is an argument about priorities and curricula.

3. In fulfilling that core purpose, it is essential that the system is well informed on future employment needs and requirements. A successful market depends on informed demand, and the labour market is no different. Individuals need high quality information on labour market opportunities, change and development, in order to make informed choices; learning providers and funders need high quality labour market information in order to set priorities, allocate resources and shape provision.

4. National occupational standards and qualifications will be UK-wide in scope, benchmarked against international standards, flexible and fit for purpose for both industry, and for the varying needs of different learners and employers. Quality will be assured in a way that minimises the burden on the individual and employer, and is focused on demonstrating the capability of the individual to employ their skills to a high standard in the real world.

5. Learning provision and assessment will be offered in a highly flexible way that recognises the circumstances of full-time, part-time and work-based

learners. It will offer choice and diversity by time, pace, place and mode of learning to maximise opportunities for all young people and adults to participate and succeed.

6. In particular, if our future dependency on upskilling and reskilling adults is to be addressed, then we must develop modes of partnership working between employers and colleges/providers that brings far closer collaboration between the learning institutions and the workplace.

7. Finally, the underlying funding of the system needs to recognise that no national exchequer can afford to bear the full costs of both a foundation learning system for young people, and a lifelong learning system serving adults. The responsive twenty-first century education and training system will be funded through balanced investments from the state, employer and individual, according to their needs and the benefits achieved by each. At an international conference in Finland in May 2005, a number of countries estimated that if the public exchequer were to have to bear the full costs of both the foundation and lifelong learning systems, they may have to almost double the share of GDP allocated to education to a point approaching 10 per cent. (The UK proportion of GDP allocated to education is currently around 5.3 per cent).

These challenges are significant and difficult, but the seeds of solutions to many of them are well understood and, in some cases, even hesitantly under way. We know they are technically feasible. The biggest issues are of will, of culture and history, but not of practicality or technical feasibility.

Before examining potential barriers to success, and offering my proposals for positive change in the system, let me explore the issue of public investment in learning at the national level.

Public investment in education

Based on purchasing power parity conversions, the UK annual expenditure per student across primary to tertiary education sits just below the OECD mean, and ranks sixteenth out of 26 nations. Examining primary, secondary and tertiary expenditure shows the same pattern for each – expenditure just below the OECD mean.[5]

Whether this is where the UK wishes to position its expenditure on education and training in the world league tables is a matter for politicians, rather than analysts. However, at a time in which all the economic evidence points to a need for nations to increase their investment in skills, it is legitimate to ask whether the evidence of spending trends shown in Figure 1.31 is an indicator of joined-up policy.

Investment – Change in national spend

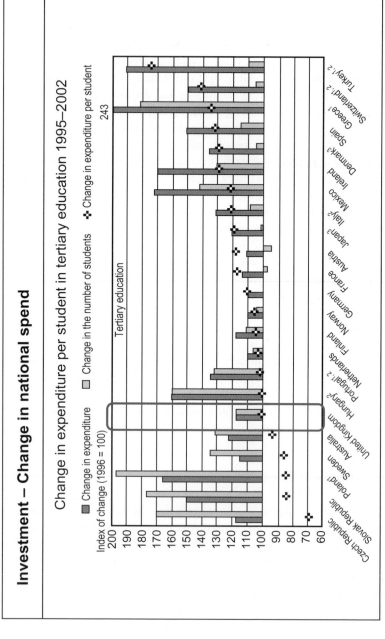

Figure 1.31 Tertiary education – change in national spending
Source: OECD, Education at a Glance, 2005, Chart B1.7

Over the period from 1995 to 2002, the UK, from a position already in the bottom half of OECD expenditure levels, and with adult participation levels also below the norm, had the lowest rate of increase in public expenditure per tertiary student in the OECD. Between 1995 and 2001, UK expenditure per tertiary student actually declined.[6] In seeking to increase the contribution to investment in skills from employers and individuals, government will also be expected to demonstrate that the exchequer is shouldering an appropriate share of funding. (See section on tripartite responsibility below.)

Potential barriers to success

Aside from the issue of funding (which I return to below), what are the key barriers to success that must be overcome if we are to build an education and training system that will support our goals for economic competitiveness?

- I highlighted on page 26 that a critical challenge for UK businesses is to raise their game, in the face of global competition from developing economies, to move towards higher skill, higher added value business models that create a true competitive edge. Mere advocacy of such a change will not produce it, and insufficient business ambition to move 'up market' will dramatically impede progress.
- Figures 1.6, 1.7 and 1.8 set out the clear evidence that investment in skills increases productivity and competitiveness, and that skills should be seen as corporate assets – making true sense of the phrase 'human capital'. Yet the majority of employers still see skills and training as costs to be reduced, rather than as assets that create genuine competitive advantage. Government

---

Potential barriers to success

- ✪ Insufficient business ambition for high value added
- ✪ Employers/government see skills as costs, not assets
- ✪ Failure to engage (all) adults in lifelong learning
  – and address basic skills shortfalls to enable participation
- • Continuing narrow-minded academic bias and elitism
- • Lack of portability of skills and qualifications
- • 'Asset poaching' and a low skilled underclass
  – importing skills from developing countries
- • Belief in the zero-sum game

Figure 1.32 Potential barriers to success

too treats training as a cost, in its tax treatment of corporate investment in skills, and the removal of earlier tax incentives for individual investment in training and education.

- The demographic analysis above confirms the importance of engaging all adults in ensuring their skills are fit for continuing employability through what will almost certainly be longer working lives. Yet research on adults with low skills in the 1990s found that 50 per cent of them said that nothing would induce them to enter formal learning again. Failure to convince a significant proportion of these 'refuseniks' to re-engage in learning will endanger our future economic growth.

- Whilst the position has improved somewhat in recent years (see successive Treasury Budget Reports, parliamentary bills, salary levels, media coverage and business calls for change around vocational skills), there still remains in Britain a significant academic elitism, and a strong element of disdain for practical vocational skills and occupations. So, despite the growing requirement for a balanced workforce, public opinion still assigns lower status and respect to practical learning.

- Both jobs and labour are becoming increasingly mobile, and it will be increasingly important that people are able to 'carry' their skills with them in recognisable ways to opportunities as they occur. There are significant discussions occurring in Europe aimed at increasing the portability of qualifications, at the same time as the four nations in the UK show signs of building incompatible qualification frameworks. If we are unable to construct a common system between the four nations here, it bodes poorly for our capability to contribute to and participate in a portable European qualifications framework.

- Many sectors and employers in the UK have proposed that the answer to our skills challenges lies in immigration, particularly from less developed countries. At the same time as a key national priority (through the Sector Skills Councils) is to encourage companies to train, rather than poach from competitors, there seems to be a belief that poaching the very skills developing countries need for their own future success is an acceptable international development strategy. Aside from the understandably growing objections from developing countries (sufficiently significant to impact on the recent G8 agenda in Edinburgh), the problem with such a policy is that it increases the potential for high levels of social exclusion by blocking future work opportunities for the low-skilled adults at whom so much UK skills policy is directed.

- The justification given for such 'asset-stripping' of developing countries has often been that there is only 'so much economy to go round', and anything goes in the fight for the UK's share. This final barrier, the belief that the global economy is a zero-sum game, will drive very different policy approaches than a belief that the world economy can grow to accommodate the needs of nations at different stages of development. The former will increase international tension, underpins much of the protectionism being seen in current World Trade discussions, and fuels anti-globalisation protests; building policies to ensure the latter belief triumphs will actually increase global harmony as well as creating more opportunities for everyone.

It is essential that policies and strategies devised to address the UK's skills challenges recognise, and include approaches that break down, or at least minimise, the impact of these barriers to success.

Priority initiatives for success

In order to address some of these challenges in England, the government launched its Skills Strategy in 2002. The Skills Strategy has received endorsement from many quarters, and many of the initiatives are beginning to make an impact on adult and employer engagement in learning. But the analysis presented here suggests that, whilst sound insofar as it goes, the Skills Strategy in its current form does not address many of the longer term challenges.

The Chancellor has commissioned Lord Leitch to investigate the skills challenges facing the UK in 2020, and much of the analysis in this report has already been presented to Lord Leitch as part of City & Guilds contribution to his thinking.

Priority initiatives for success

A. Tripartite responsibility – devise/implement the policy

B. Maximise youth success – learning for the 100%

C. Engaging employers
  - Sectoral campaigns, strategies, qualifications, priorities
  - Cluster and special programmes for SMEs
  - Reporting standards and incentives – treat skills as assets!
  - Public funding prioritised on 'economic and social utility'

D. Engaging adults
  - Information advice and guidance + coherent LMI
  - Entitlements to appropriate levels and needs
  - 'Licences to practise'
  - Individual Learning Accounts (real ones!)

Figure 1.33 Priority initiatives for success

Detailed below is a series of ten proposals that may help the UK to anticipate and respond to these challenges, and ensure a secure future for our people, our businesses and our economy.

1. Tripartite responsibility for skills

I argue on page 33 that the overall costs of a comprehensive foundation learning system (for young people) and a multiple access lifelong learning system (for adults) would inevitably exceed the capacity of any nation's exchequer to pay. The Skills Task Force argued in 2000 that the answer had to lie in identifying and agreeing the key principles of an agreement for shared responsibility for skills between the state, employers and individuals.[7] To put the issue more simply, who pays?

The Task Force set out a first attempt to define the responsibilities of those three key beneficiaries of the learning system in the following terms:

'**Individuals** should take responsibility for reviewing their skills and initiating action to keep their employability skills up to date. They should cooperate fully with their employer in job-specific training designed to meet business objectives, and those who can afford to should make a reasonable contribution to the time and costs of transferable learning to improve their continuing employability.

'**Employers** should plan, deliver and evaluate the effectiveness of learning for all their employees to meet their business objectives. They should bear the full costs of job-specific learning, and contribute through encouragement, support and investment to developing the transferable skills and continuing employability of their staff commensurate with the benefits which accrue to them by so doing. They should cooperate through sector training bodies to assess their future skills needs, and inform and support providers in meeting those needs.

'**Government** should assess the learning needed to achieve national economic and social objectives, and take lead responsibility for ensuring that the education and training system is equipped to meet those needs. It should ensure that all citizens have equitable opportunities to obtain a minimum foundation of learning for their future employability, and contribute to the costs of continuing learning, through fees, grants or loans, according to economic priority and individual need.'

These proposals argued, in short, that the state, employers and individuals should contribute to the costs of lifelong learning in proportions commensurate with the benefits gained – what is required now is the development of those principles into a formal policy, agreed with employers and unions, which sets out who should bear what share of costs for learning at different levels and stages of working life.

The time is right for the government to initiate a public debate on these issues, leading to the establishment of a formal protocol of tripartite responsibility for skills and lifelong learning.

2. Public funding prioritised to 'utility'.

As well as agreeing the principles of tripartite responsibility, there needs to be a clear policy on how public funding allocated to education is spent. At the moment, public funding for adult learning is driven heavily by individual demand; rightly or wrongly, it is seen as a key part of the UK liberal education tradition. Such a policy is fine when there are sufficient public resources available to meet adult demand, as there generally was until the 1990s, when the real need for adults to regularly update their skills for continuing employability became clearer – confirming the economic, in addition to the social, value of lifelong learning.

Proposal 1 above, on tripartite responsibility, sets out an agenda to establish adult and employer contributions to learning; this initiative is concerned with setting the priorities applied to public funding in further and higher education.

The principle behind the use of public funding for most non-educational purposes is clear – the state should invest in such a way as to maximise the return to the nation from such investment. If productivity and competitiveness are key national goals, and if learning and skills are a key tool to improve productivity and competitiveness, then public funding should be more clearly targeted on skills for employment, and the public subsidy in other lower-priority learning reduced as necessary to support that.

The public agrees. A MORI poll, published in November 2005, found that most adults did not realise how much government subsidy was included in further education course fees (typically around 70–75 per cent or more). When told, 84 per cent of the public said they thought adults should pay at least 50 per cent of the costs of non-work-related learning; 60 per cent even thought adults should bear the full cost. In the same month, the Foster Review proposed that the primary purpose of the further education system should be providing skills for employment, and argued that public funding should be prioritised on that basis.

Of course, what's covered by the phrase 'priority learning' must be broadly defined – and include basic skills, employability programmes, access and taster programmes for the low-skilled, an adult entitlement to Level 2, Level 3 and higher full vocational programmes, other courses in SSC's Sector Qualification Strategies, and many degree and post-graduate programmes.

And the need for our education system to enhance both economic competitiveness and social cohesion argues against a simple and narrow employment focus for funding in education, and in favour of developing a new principle for prioritising educational funding – what might be called 'economic and social utility'. How can public funding for all post-school education best be utilised to produce the most positive impact on economic competitiveness and social inclusion?

Priorities and requirements that are of maximum 'utility' will vary over time, by sector, geographically and by category of individual, and so policy provision will need to be made to monitor and update the funding system over time to reflect such changes in requirements.

Alongside a public debate on tripartite funding responsibility, there should be a wide discussion on how public funding for education should itself be prioritised according to 'economic and social utility', agreeing the principles of what constitutes such 'utility' for use by both the Learning and Skills Council, and the Higher Education Funding Council for England, in allocating future public funding to institutions and learning programmes.

3. Maximising Youth Success.

Since the 1944 Education Act, England has developed a school education system which, after 61 years, still fails half of our young people at 16. Only 51 per cent of young people achieve what is considered to be the basic benchmark for completing Year 11 – five GCSEs at grades A*–C. From birth, the human animal's natural state is learning. Young people learn (to do) more in the first five years of their life – to walk, talk, listen, understand, draw, create, socialise, use tools, etc. – than we even recognise; the hunger for learning in their second five years is also extraordinary. Yet six years later, half of our young people have apparently failed, and many have lost the will to learn within the formal system. The fundamental truth is that it is not the young people who are failures, but a system that is failing to educate half our population.

It is also important to remember that in the earlier heydays of apprenticeships (the 1960s to early 1980s), when entry to university was only available to the top 10–12 per cent of young people, the vast majority of apprentices were drawn from the cohort that today are also entering higher education programmes. The young apprentices of this century are, to a significant extent, drawn from a cohort which has achieved significantly less in their school education than their predecessors of 20 years earlier, and this is noticeably impacting on apprenticeship success rates. It is not that these young people are actually capable of less, but that their level of prior attainment often requires a more supportive learning environment to achieve the same levels of success.

The last 15–20 years of the national curriculum has seen the progressive 'academicisation' of the curriculum, as all practical learning has been systematically eliminated. Young people for whom practical or applied learning is more suited have found less and less in the school system that plays to their talents, and have been marginalised and branded as failures. At the same time, employers claim that young people coming (successfully) through the academic system are less and less well prepared for the world of work, that their generic skills in communication, number and collaborative working are poor, and they have too little capacity to apply their learning to real world problems.

It is time for a fundamental restructuring of the secondary school system to serve the needs of **all** young people, not just the academically able, and to separate university recruitment from the school assessment regime. Summative assessment in the school system should be designed to testify to the individual's readiness for the world of work and adult life, and their capacity to continue learning in their preferred mode and styles. Suitability to progress to higher levels of academic study should not be the only measure of achievement or success, and universities should be required to recognise a wider set of definitions of success for entry to higher education, as well as adapt more of their provision to serve 'economic and social utility' (ref. Proposal 2 above).

The full Tomlinson proposals, which attracted extraordinary unanimity across the education and training system, abolishing GCSEs and A-levels, and offering the core as specified and breadth and choice across the full spectrum of general and vocational provision should be fully implemented for all young people.

4. Sectoral action with employers.

In 2000, the Skills Task Force challenged the government and industry to review the role of National Training Organisations (NTOs) with a view to creating more dynamic organisations, deeply engaged with their industries, and with the resources, support and capacity to increase training, raise skill levels and thus enhance the productivity and competitiveness of their sectors.

The resultant Sector Skills Councils (SSCs) are finally coming of age, with many already strongly engaged with the leading businesses in their sectors, developing skills foresight programmes, supporting employers towards leading edge practice in training and development, and helping to devise new occupational standards and qualifications that are fit for the twenty-first century.

Whilst we are still undoubtedly some distance away from a fully credible national network of SSCs, it is increasingly clear that good SSCs can have the transformational effects hoped for. Significant effort needs to be put in completing the coverage of all key sectors with highly capable and successful SSCs so that all employers can be supported to improve. In the meantime, government should provide the time, resources, encouragement and support to allow the system to bed down and improve, but resist the temptation to fundamentally upend the system and risk yet again losing employer credibility and engagement.

At the same time, SSCs must now redouble their efforts to engage industry in their work, promote the benefits of training to productivity and competitiveness, research the future skills needs of the sector, assist companies to introduce world class practice, and support the education and training system to better respond to future employment requirements and opportunities.

5. Cluster programmes for SMEs.

Almost three-quarters of the UK workforce are employed within the 3 per cent of employers with more than 50 staff (Figures 1.28 and 1.29), and so it is right that a significant amount of focused effort should be directed at the larger firms.

However, not only do smaller firms with less than 50 employees still employ over a third of the workforce, other research confirms that the skill levels of staff in smaller firms are significantly lower than those working in larger organisations. So the skills challenges faced by individuals working in smaller firms is often greater, there are far more of such firms and they are significantly more difficult to reach.

The British Chambers of Commerce in 2000 surveyed over 3,000 of its member companies, and found that only 20 per cent of firms with less than 50 employees had any manager with knowledge or responsibility for personnel, training or development issues, and only one in five of those had a full-time responsible manager – in short, only 4 per cent of small firms have a full time HR/training manager. On the other hand, 71 per cent of firms with over 50 employees had a full-time personnel and training manager.[8]

So not only do smaller firms face larger skills challenges, they lack the internal resources to be able to deal with this themselves. The problem for SSCs and other bodies is that it is easy to see how 25 sector bodies might reach the 37,000 50+ firms; it is far more difficult to conceive how they might reach the 1.2 million smaller businesses.

The answer appears to lie in 'clusters'. Both the British Chambers of Commerce and the Federation of Small Businesses estimated (in 2000) that approximately 80 per cent of all small firms were located in 'clusters' of one form or another – mostly geographical, through business parks, industrial estates or the high street. Many of these, and others, also work in supply chain clusters to larger firms, and so can be reached collectively through carefully designed cluster initiatives, bringing together local and sectoral organisations through effective partnership working. There were many programmes operated by the Training and Enterprise Councils (TECs) during 1994–97 that fully demonstrated the efficacies of geographical and supply-chain cluster schemes for SMEs. Most operated by creating learning centres in business parks, industrial estates, or large contracting firms, and using peripatetic trainers to bring learning into/near the workplace, serving the combined needs of what can often be a thousand or more staff within each cluster. (These programmes were part of the legacy of TECs that were lost during the transition from TECs to the Learning and Skills Council.)

There were similarities in these cluster programmes to aspects of the recent Employer Training Pilots, but with significantly lower public investment, and significantly lower deadweight. It is time to re-instigate regional cluster-based skills programmes for SMEs, through integrated working between Sector Skills Councils, regional Learning and Skills Councils, and the Regional Development Agencies.

6. Reporting, incentives and employers.

The research by Bassi Investments on the return from training investment to shareholder value (Figure 1.7) demonstrates clearly the benefits to corporate bottom lines and investors of an effective corporate training programme. That return clearly reinforces how appropriate at times the phrase 'human capital' can be (though it can also be used demeaningly).

In their full article, Bassi Investments argue that amending company reporting requirements to include a section on skills investment would change investor practice, and cause increasing numbers of institutional investors to favour companies that invest in training. There is a strong correlation between systematic investor demand and company behaviour – if investment increased, and share value and profitability rose from training investment, companies would start investing more in training, and ensure that they got full value from that investment.

Whether changes to corporate reporting requirements would have that effect needs further investigation, as does the suggestion from many quarters of some form of tax incentives for firms who implement sound training practices, e.g. through the Investors in People standard.

The Skills Task Force certainly believed that such schemes would increase motivation and change practice amongst smaller firms, and included it as one of their final recommendations.

What the UK does need to do, and such schemes can help with, is to begin to change the perception of training in businesses from being a cost to being an asset. Assets are protected and their value maximised, costs are cut and are seen as an unnecessary evil. Given the highly sceptical attitude to training of many UK firms, particularly small and medium companies, this is a goal worthy of pursuit.

The Treasury should work with the CBI, SSCs, the accountancy profession and other business organisations to investigate options for new reporting standards, tax schemes and incentives, and other mechanisms that can assist with repositioning skills as key assets in the corporate environment.

7. Labour market information and guidance.

Consumer and economic research confirms that one of the key factors in the successful operation of any market is informed demand. The labour market is no different – ensuring the availability of labour with the right skills at the right time is essential for its optimal operation, and this is fundamentally dependent upon choices made by young people and adults, and the availability of sufficient training places in the supply side.

The Skills Task Force highlighted in its third report in 1999 that, whilst the UK spent significant sums on research into a wide spectrum of labour market data, that data was not comprehensive in its coverage, inconsistent in its data definitions, sectoral and geographical datasets did not correlate, and key national data on employers and the labour force needed improving to enable better disaggregation by either geography or sector.

Many significant improvements have been made in the last six years. Developments of the *Labour Force Survey*, the creation of the *National Employer Skills Survey*, and the *Skills in England* and *Working Futures* reports have all genuinely enhanced the quality of data and high level analysis available. The new sectoral analyses and reports from the Sector Skills Councils, coordinated through the Sector Skills Development Agency, will provide increasingly richer data over the next three years.

But to impact on the forward planning inside a college, or to be able to help a 17- or a 42-year-old make an important learning or career choice, that data needs translating into very accessible information and communications available in their language, through their media and when they need it.

The UK needs a much more effective, well informed and professional careers information, advice and guidance service, supported by a national interactive website of diagnostic, information and advisory functions that makes such all-age support nationally available.

The technology to create such an Internet-based system is now widely available and understood, and the data sources needed to inform it are described above, and can be extended to meet requirements as the system evolves. That system could then provide the key background information service to support locally-tailored and locally-based adult information advice and guidance services to offer additional guidance and counselling support where required.

8. Entitlements and Skills priorities

An essential part of developing a policy on tripartite responsibility for skills between the state, employers and individuals will be to set out the key principles for the use of public funding component of the total costs.

It is taken as a given (in this paper) that the state will continue to fully fund a state pre-school and school system for all young people up to the age of 16. But what policies apply beyond that point? Our policy on the funding of young people's learning remains confused and inconsistent, with different policies applying to young people in colleges below and above 19, to apprentices up to and over 25, and to university students.

Figure 1.21 highlighted the evidence that, whilst the UK has increased skill levels amongst young people by age 21 to levels comparable with our European competitors, by age 25–28 the gap has widened again. If we wish to close our youth skills gap, we need to extend the opportunity for young people to continue in learning, through an entitlement for every young person to attain skills up to at least Level 3. By 2010, the majority of new jobs will require Level 3 skills – this must become the expected standard of attainment for all young people by age 25. Government should establish that standard through an entitlement for all young people to fully-funded Level 3 training up to the age of 25, either through colleges, training providers or apprenticeships.

The demographic trends make it essential that we increase the stock of higher skilled adult workers, as well as draw more non-employed adults into the workforce. I argue on page 16 that, under a tripartite responsibility for skills, the government 'should ensure that all citizens have equitable opportunities to obtain a minimum foundation of learning for their future employability', and the current Level 2 entitlement for adults to basic skills and their first Level 2 qualification implements that principle.

Beyond those entitlements (which could themselves be 'upgraded' over time), employers and adults should normally be expected to contribute to the costs of learning in a way that links their level of investment to the level of benefit received. In special cases, government could choose to extend the concept of entitlements to cover higher level training in sectoral or regional priority areas to respond to significant economic or social need.

9. 'Licences to practise'

It is an extraordinary characteristic of the UK that we are happy to regulate the skills and capabilities of our so-called professional classes (lawyers, doctors, accountants, engineers, etc.) setting minimum standards for qualifications, experience and continuing professional development, but we do not expect the same of our skilled craftsmen and women, technicians, or trades people.

Apparently, it is acceptable in the UK for unqualified people to lay our railway tracks; look after our elderly relatives in care homes; rewire or replumb our houses; handle and prepare food in restaurants and factories; all despite the huge risks to health and safety. And then we wonder why there are so many cowboys operating in the market, and why the actual skills of so many of the workers that enter our homes are so low.

Even the recent influx of highly skilled workers from eastern Europe, praised for the quality of their work and their customer service, hasn't led us to recognise that the difference is that in Eastern Europe (and the rest of Europe, the US, Canada and most of the developed world), these trades are licensed, and no-one can call themselves, for example, an electrician, or practise that craft, without being qualified to specified levels and subject to registration.

It is ironic that the Institute of Plumbing and Heating Engineers has fought unsuccessfully for one hundred years to introduce a registration scheme for plumbers. They know that their reputation as a trade, and the health and safety of the population, depends on high quality work performed by individuals who take their trade seriously. Yet it has been successive governments that have opposed such a scheme, proclaiming the interests of the populace are better served without such an assurance of quality and safety.

The evidence from around the world is clear: licence to practise schemes work. They raise skill levels, increase respect for those occupations, improve quality and workmanship, provide a level playing field for good companies, reduce or even eliminate 'cowboys' and increase public confidence. It is time they were extended to all crafts and trades in the UK that impact upon public health and safety, or upon consumer protection and confidence.

10. Individual learning accounts

My previous proposals argue that skills are essential for economic growth and individual employability, and that individuals may need upskilling or reskilling at various stages during their adult life. The principle of tripartite responsibility rightly places some of the responsibility for such personal development on the individual, since they will normally benefit through increased earning capacity.

But individuals cannot easily predict when skills development will be essential for their future employability – with shocks like redundancy, recession, or technological change affecting most people at some stage during their lifetime. For maximum labour market efficiency, individuals will need to be able to pursue learning when the time is right for them, and be able to locate the resources to support such learning when necessary.

The Scottish Lifelong Learning Committee's report some years ago recommended that each citizen should have an entitlement to so many hours of publicly funded learning throughout their lifetime, almost as a credit to be drawn down over time.

Establishing such a 'credit' concept in the education system was one aspect of the original idea for Individual Learning Accounts, developed during the early years of the current administration. The principle was simple. If, in a lifelong learning society, individuals needed to be able to access new learning for skills at various stages of over their 30–40-year working lives, then society needed a mechanism to ensure that the resources to support that would be available when required.

The individual learning account would support maximum flexibility for adults through three elements: a 'credit' on the learning system for so much publicly-funded learning time in a lifetime; the capacity to save, tax free, for learning in the future; and the capacity for deferred borrowing on advantageous terms (like the current student loans system). During the developmental thinking on ILAs from 1997 to 1999, this was often referred to as 'credit to learn, save to learn, borrow to learn'.

The system of so-called Individual Learning Accounts introduced by the DfES in 2000 bore little resemblance to the original concept, and lacked sufficient basic controls to prevent predictable fraud. These mistakes did not invalidate the full ILA concept, and the arguments for it today are as strong as they ever were.

Conclusion

The skills challenges facing the UK are becoming increasingly well understood:

- too many young people disengaging from learning and skills at age 16 (if not 14);
- major demographic changes occurring over the next 15 years, fundamentally changing the shape of the UK workforce, and making us more dependent on the skills of the existing population of working age;

- rising skill levels required in all occupations;
- inadequate publicly accessible information on future labour market changes, and the balance of skills required for our future economy;
- too few people pursuing essential craft, technical and trade skills at intermediate levels, leading to worsening skills shortages over the next ten years;
- a serious imbalance in public policy and public opinion on the need for academic versus practical learning;
- too many adults with low skills and poor levels of literacy and numeracy;
- the need to increase the volume and level of education and training in the UK beyond the capacity of the state to pay.

What is certain is that a policy of 'more of the same', or even of slow evolutionary improvements, will simply not produce the radical change in skills and productivity that is essential for the UK's continuing economic competitiveness and for ensuring a more inclusive society for all citizens.

The importance of getting skills right for the future of our nation and our people is gaining increasing public and political recognition, with successive White Papers, Treasury reports, and now the Leitch Review of skills requirements up to 2020. Work arising from the Skills Task Force and the subsequent Skills Strategy has begun to have a visible impact on adult basic skills, apprenticeships, participation in intermediate vocational skills, and employer engagement, but the hill we still have to climb is steep.

We must recognise the value of high level, high quality skills to our economy and our people, raise our sights beyond competence to excellence, celebrate and reward excellence in skills and training, and establish the UK again as a nation where our whole workforce is renowned for being genuinely world class.

The time is right for another step change in policy and strategy, building on recent success, but with renewed innovation, energy, focus and commitment. I hope the proposals outlined above might contribute to making that step change a substantial and successful one.

Notes

1 Friedman, T., 'It's a Flat World After All', *The New York Times*, 3 April 2005.
2 A definition popularised by the Department of Trade and Industry's Innovation Unit in the 1990s.
3 Wallace, P. (2001) *'Agequake: Riding the Demographic Rollercoaster Shaking Business, Finance and our World'*, Nicholas Brealey: London.
4 DfES (2003) *Education and Skills: The Economic Benefits*, p. 17.

5 OECD, *Education at a Glance 2005*, Charts B1.1 and B1.2, p. 158–162.
6 OECD, *Education at a Glance 2004*, Chart B1.7, p. 212.
7 National Skills Task Force (2000) *Skills for All: Proposals for a National Skills Agenda*, London: DfES, p. 64.
8 The reason is simple. As smaller firms grow, their primary focus is on the next contract, the next sale. It is only when the business is more established, and the order book is more secure, that most small firms can actually afford to bring in 'administrative managers' with the roles described here. The growth point of 50 employees seems to be a watershed for personnel/training managers. (The author was Director General of the British Chambers of Commerce when this research was conducted.)

CHAPTER 2

Skills and social productivity

LEON FEINSTEIN AND RICARDO SABATES

Introduction

This paper describes findings from the last seven years of research by the Centre for Research of the Wider Benefits of Learning, which was set up in 1999 by the Department for Education and Employment, as it then was, based on the recognition that education has wider benefits. In other words, education is not only about developing economic productivity and economic growth, jobs and employment, but also has wider implications for the lives of individuals, families and society. Although the existence of the wider benefits of education has been argued since the time of Ancient Greece (see Weiss, 1995), empirical evidence to support that argument in a modern context is limited and there are not clear conceptual frameworks for clarifying both the wider outcomes of education and the mechanisms by which education may impact upon such outcomes. For this reason, the work of the Centre has focused on understanding the multiple ways in which learning may impact upon wider outcomes, modelling and measuring the impact of learning, and translating this impact in monetary terms in order to inform government departments about the broader returns to investments in education.

Learning should not be reduced to education provided by schools or higher education institutions. There are important benefits to adult learning. For example, work-based adult training has important economic returns (Blundell, Dearden and Meghir, 1996; Feinstein, Galindo-Rueda and Vignoles, 2004), achieving qualifications during adulthood improves women's chances of re-entering into the labour market (Jenkins *et al.,* 2003; Jenkins, 2006), participation in adult learning has positive effects on chances in smoking, exercise taken, and life satisfaction (Feinstein and Hammond, 2004). However, a wider definition of learning does not mean just adult learning, but lifelong learning. To this end, the focus of our work has been on trying to understand the relative roles of learning at different ages, the ways in which educational provision, in its broadest sense, can support people and communities in having lifetime experiences of learning, and the benefits of those experiences.

Our basic argument for the wider benefits of learning is that qualifications matter, basic skills matter, vocational skills matter and academic skills matter. However, there are also other wider skills that are often neglected and which are not only important in the labour market, but also in the formation of basic skills and for the achievement of qualifications. These wider skills may have essential implications for the wellbeing of individuals and society. Therefore, to focus only on achievement of qualifications as an immediate outcome of learning understates the role that learning can play in the lives of individuals and communities. This paper aims to classify the immediate outcomes of learning, puts forward a model for the understanding of how learning impacts on outcomes, reviews some of the empirical evidence on the impacts of education on wider outcomes and concludes with the implications of the work of the Centre for public policy.

A threefold classification of the immediate outcomes of learning

Immediate outcomes of learning can be classified into three different groups:

- skills, competencies and beliefs
- social networks
- qualifications.

These immediate outcomes are ontologically different and, although there are important links between them, need to be treated separately.

Skills, competencies and beliefs

Skills, competencies and beliefs are features of the individual. They include a very wide range of cognitive skills, technical and vocational skills, social and communication skills, resilience and self-concepts. In human capital theory education is an implicit investment that leads to labour productivity through enhancement of skills and competencies that are of value in the production of goods and services. These skills need not be clearly defined in specific terms a priori as the theory is general in nature, emphasising that what is of value in economic production will earn a wage return in proportion to its marginal productivity. However, standard economic analyses emphasise the importance of cognitive ability, technical skills and soft skills, such as social and communication skills.

Resilience is a construct describing positive adaptation in the face of adversity (Schoon and Bynner, 2003). It is not a personality attribute, but rather a process of positive adaptation in response to significant adversity or trauma (Luthar, Cicchetti, and Becker, 2000). For example, the experience of disadvantage early in life for less resilient individuals may weaken their ability to adapt to future challenges (Brooks-Gunn, 1995).

Self-concepts concern an individual's perception of themselves, such as of their own abilities and worth. They depend on the information available to the individual and the cognitive ability to process this information (Markus and Wurf, 1987). Self-concepts are multi-dimensional (Shavelson and Marsh, 1986) varying across a range of different domains, for example relating to academic capabilities, social capabilities, or general self-worth. Self-concepts develop whilst children are at school. Amongst very young children, self-concept is consistently high, but with increasing life experience children learn their relative strengths and weaknesses. In general, their level of self-concept declines, becomes more differentiated with age, and becomes more highly correlated with external indicators of competence, such as skills, accomplishments, and the opinions of significant others (Marsh, 1985; Marsh, 1990; Shavelson and Marsh, 1986).

The belief or perception, for example, that school and learning is unpleasant is a barrier to lifelong learning. Adults with previous negative or unpleasant experiences of learning are not likely to engage in learning unless they believe that they are able to learn and that if something is confusing does not mean that it is impossible to understand. For these adults, their learning experiences in adulthood should also be about unlearning, learning that redresses or changes individuals' perceptions towards learning. The more adult learning can redress this balance the more successful the experience will be in creating positive learning outcomes for those most disadvantaged by prior experiences of learning. This is not about the acquisition of qualifications, although related to it in important ways.

In summary, skills, competencies and beliefs are features of the individual that are impacted by learning in very complex ways and with very important implications for learning outcomes.

Social networks

Social networks are distinct to skills, competencies and beliefs in that a network is not a feature of an individual, but a feature of society. Social networks have been conceptualised in terms of different forms of social capital (Coleman, 1990; Putnam, 1995). The most basic form of social capital is bonding social capital, which coalesces around a single, shared identity, and tends to reinforce the confidence and homogeneity of a particular group. Bridging social capital refers to horizontal social networks that extend beyond homogenous groups. This form of social capital involves cross-cutting networks amongst people of various ethnic, cultural, and socio-demographic backgrounds. Linking social capital is characterised by connections with individuals and institutions with power and authority. This is theorised in terms of vertical rather than horizontal networks within social hierarchies.

We take the view that the phrase social capital is important in focusing attention on the transaction between an individual and his/her social network, and that the form that the social network takes has huge implications for individuals' lives. An important aspect of the educational experience is that it involves the engagement of individuals in collective experiences of learning and development. This can have positive and negative effects, bringing benefits but also risks. One of the key influences of education may be in terms of changes to the social networks in which individuals take part, as well as to the ways in which they develop and maintain such networks. Educational settings may be a source of support or distress depending on the nature of the relationships formed in them. Education has the capability to promote social integration and civic engagement, and to widen social networks.

Qualifications

Qualifications are classified separately here because they are not a feature of the individual, they are something that an individual earns and possesses and can use as a signal in the labour market or as a signal to themselves about their own capabilities. Qualifications can also be a signal to others, but they are not an actual attribute, they are not a feature of an individual. In other words, an individual has a qualification; she is not a qualification.

Individuals earn qualifications from some experiences of learning and not from others and those qualifications are then very important in their interactions in social networks and in economic transactions. Qualifications can also reflect individuals' attainment, so they provide an indication of the ability to learn, as well as indicating perseverance and the ability to accomplish tasks or assignments. Qualifications may also be summary indicators of learning but they do not equate to the learning experience. Qualifications may also indicate acquisition of skills, especially for vocational qualifications. For the labour market, qualifications are signals to employers of what individuals might have achieved and may proxy for forms of social advantage. They indicate that individuals have mastered what was taught and produced what was expected of them, which are valuable tools for labour market success. Qualifications are not always well understood and they are measured with error.

Empirical evidence on the role of the immediate outcomes of learning

Figures 2.1 to 2.3 show the relationship between some attributes of individuals at age ten and some features of adult life, measured at age 30, controlling for a wide range of family background at age ten. This empirical evidence conditions out the impact of social class, number of children in the household, the type of housing, mother's mental health, parental interest in education, parental education itself, and other wide range features of the child's experience at aged ten. It then uses seven features of child's capabilities at age ten and investigates which of these capabilities are most predictive of adult life success.

Predicted changes in probability of not obtaining Level 4; by age ten capabilities, men

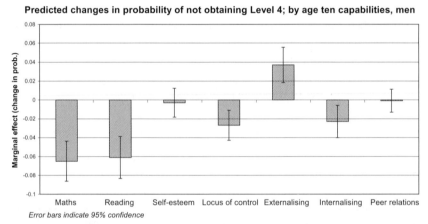

Error bars indicate 95% confidence

Figure 2.1 The bars represent the predicted change in the probability of not achieving Level 4 qualifications by age 30. Main factors measured at age ten are maths and reading test scores, self-esteem, locus of control, externalising and internalising behaviours, and good peer relations. *Data source*: 1970 British Cohort Study

The focus of much of the education system has been on maths and reading because there is the view that maths and reading are particularly important for adult life success. Here we explore three outcomes at age 30 using information from the 1970 British Cohort Study: lack of achieving Level 4 qualifications, being in a workless household with children, and history of criminality. These outcomes are all expressed in a negative way, in the sense of a feature of social exclusion, and the aim is to compare the relative importance of maths and reading in predicting these features of social exclusion with five other features of child development at age ten.

Among these features of development we include self-esteem, peer relations and locus of control (defined by the sense that children believe that events happen because of their own influence as opposed to random chance or external factors). We also include externalising and internalising behaviours, which are both indications of self-regulation. We argue that alongside maths and reading, self-regulation is a basic skill. The ability to function socially and manage emotional distress without disturbing social relationships is a basic skill that individuals need to have in order to function effectively in society and to have successful adult lives.

Externalising and internalising behaviours in the 1970 Cohort study were assessed by the teacher when the child was ten years of age. Both of these measures are indicative of emotional distress. The correlation between externalising and internalising behaviour is 0.54, so externalisers tend also to be internalisers and vice versa. Externalising behaviour can be defined by acting up in the classroom; being naughty, bullying other children, stealing things, fidgeting, hitting other children; and internalising behaviour, by going quiet or not responding to the teacher.

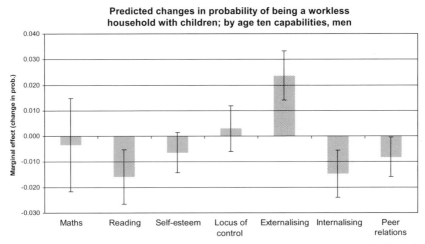

Figure 2.2 The bars represent the probability of being a workless household with children by age 30. Main factors measured at age ten are maths and reading test scores, self-esteem, locus of control, externalising and internalising behaviours, and good peer relations.
Data source: 1970 British Cohort Study. *Source*: Feinstein and Bynner (2004).

The point to highlight from these three figures is that for an academic outcome, such as not getting a degree by age 30, maths and reading are very protective against that outcome (Figure 2.1). But for the other two outcomes, workless household with children and likelihood of criminal offences, externalising behaviour is particularly important. Moreover, for the probability of offending at age 30, which is measured by being found guilty in a court of law or magistrates court more than once, maths and reading are not predictive of this outcome at all, but externalised behaviour is very predictive (Figure 2.3). We argue that this evidence suggests that self-regulation is a basic skill required to function in society.

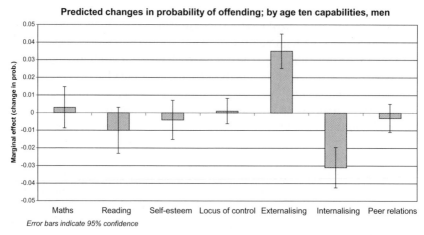

Predicted changes in probability of offending; by age ten capabilities, men

Error bars indicate 95% confidence

Figure 2.3 The bars represent the probability of committing a criminal offence by age 30. Main factors measured at age ten are maths and reading test scores, self-esteem, locus of control, externalising and internalising behaviours, and good peer relations.
Data source: 1970 British Cohort Study.

Furthermore, for living in a workless household with children, which will impact not only upon the individual but also upon his/her children, maths at age ten does not predict this outcome, reading is predictive but externalising behaviour is more predictive (Figure 2.2). This raises the question: why are we focusing so much attention in the education system on maths and reading? We do not suggest that maths and reading do not matter, and they interact in important ways in self-discipline, but we argue for the need of an education system which recognises the importance of these and other wider features of development.

A simple model for the wider benefits of learning

We have postulated that the learning experience can generate immediate outcomes such as skills, competencies and beliefs, social networks and qualifications. We also reviewed evidence showing that attributes of the individual during childhood (all of which can be immediate outcomes of the learning experience of the child) can have important associations with indicators of deprivation during adulthood. Furthermore, we showed that the association between immediate outcomes of learning and adult indicators of deprivation depends on the indicator that is being measured. We now propose a simple model for the link between learning, immediate learning outcomes and wider social outcomes.

Learning and educational experiences can generate wider benefits that are not always easily or commonly reduced to a simple monetary metric but which are nonetheless of important social value. We name this term 'social productivity', the capacity of education to support the generation of outcomes of social value. These outcomes may be thought of in positive terms as the role of education and learning in the sustaining of positive developmental trajectories or the achievement of potential, and the formation and generation of positive life chances. Alternatively social productivity may be thought about in terms of the prevention of the many negative outcomes that tend to dominate much policy discussion, in terms of aspects of individual exclusion and community breakdown such as obesity, crime, teenage parenthood, antisocial behaviour, intolerance, mental health problems, social division, disengagement, drug abuse and social immobility. Education can play a role in the prevention of most if not all of these features of personal and social dislocation, although one cannot at all assume that the role of education is always beneficial.

Figure 2.4 sets out a simple model of the mediating mechanisms for achievement and description of the social productivity or wider benefits of education. In this model the factors gained through learning are expressed in terms of

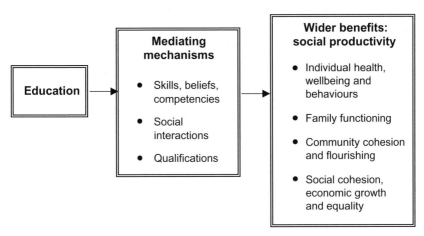

Figure 2.4 A simple model for the wider benefits of learning

three particular features of individuals and their relationships with others that we described above: skills and capabilities, social networks and qualifications. This framework is useful in part because it highlights the importance of a good understanding of the wider benefits of learning for analysing and assessing the productivity of the education system.

Figure 2.4 highlights the basic premise that education supports the expansion, formation and sustenance of a broad range of features of personal and social development. These are important for an equivalently broad set of wider benefits that are central to public policy across the whole system of government, influencing wellbeing and functioning at the level of the individual, family, community and nation. Technical and academic skills are essential for this, but so are features of personal development such as resilience, self-regulation, a positive sense of self and personal and social identity. The capability of individuals to function as civic agents with notions of personal responsibility, tolerance and respect depends on these wider features of self as well as on the interaction with others in schools, workplaces, communities, neighbourhoods and through the media and other channels.

Thus, the study of the wider benefits of learning has brought us to emphasise these wider features of personal and social development as being influenced by the education system and of under-recognised social value. Therefore, we highlight the notion of the social productivity of education, the capability of the education system in its broadest sense to contribute to wide-ranging policy objectives, provided the education system can recognise and respond to the requirements that this role places on it. In other words, education is important, not just because it is economically productive but also because it is socially productive. It brings about benefits to society and there are returns to investments in education at all stages of the life course because these social outcomes are of value to society, not always economically transacted, not always economically measurable, but nonetheless a benefit to society.

Empirical evidence on the wider benefits of learning

In this section, we review empirical literature that focuses on whether education has a causal impact on wider outcomes and the magnitude of its impact. As we will see below, most of this evidence focuses on highest qualifications attained or years of schooling as measures of education. For this reason, we also review the empirical evidence on the impact of adult education on wider outcomes.

Recent reviews of the empirical literature have demonstrated that education is a powerful predictor of wider outcomes such as personal health, lifestyles, wellbeing, children's education, parenting, acquisition of information and effective use of information, family planning, voting and civic participation, saving, adapting to technological change, among others (see reviews by Haveman and Wolfe, 1984; Grossman, 2005; Feinstein, *et al.*, 2006). Here, we focus on three examples where the causal impact of education has been estimated and the magnitude of its impact quantified.

Chevalier and Feinstein (2006) first estimated a causal effect of education on reducing the risk of depression during adulthood. Then, they simulated that the impact of policies that took women without qualifications to Level 2 in the UK would lead to a reduction in their risk of adult depression at age 42 from 26 per cent to 22 per cent, that is a reduction of 15 per cent; this population represents 17 per cent of depressed individuals. Assuming that this reduction was constant throughout the working life, and with an estimated cost of depression of £9 billion a year (Thomas and Morris, 2003), the benefit of education would be to reduce the total cost of depression for the population of interest by £200 million a year.

Evidence from the US showed that an additional year of education lowers the probability of dying in the next ten years between 1.3 to 3.6 percentage points (Lleras-Muney, 2005). In terms of life expectancy, for people in the US in 1960, one more year of education increased life expectancy at age 35 by as much as 1.7 years. Evidence from Sweden suggests that some of the effect of education on health was mediated by income, but not all (Spasojevic, 2003). In fact, education produced substantially greater effects through channels other than income. In monetary terms, the impact of education on health was translated into an increase in income that ranged between US $1,700 and US $17,700.

We now turn to the evidence around the impact of adult learning. Feinstein and Hammond (2004) carried out primary analysis of longitudinal cohort studies for the UK to consider whether experiences of adult learning are related to changes in adult life (see for example Figure 2.5). They used the 1958 cohort to examine the contribution of adult learning to a wide range of health and health behaviours. Analysis was in terms of changes between the ages of 33 and 42 years in life outcomes for adults, controlling for their development and context up to age 33. The results showed that participation in adult learning had positive effects on changes in smoking (Figure 2.5), exercise taken, and life satisfaction. Effect sizes were small in absolute terms. However, there is little change in behaviours during mid-adulthood, and relative to this baseline, participation in adult learning is an important driver for change.

Feinstein and Hammond (2004), using the methodology employed for health outcomes described above, showed that participation in adult learning had positive effects on race tolerance, authoritarian attitudes, political cynicism, political interest, number of memberships, and voting behaviour. Again, effect sizes were small, but given that there is little change in attitudes in

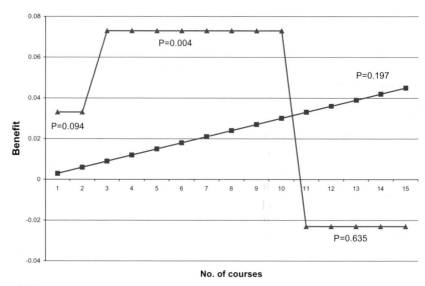

Figure 2.5 The lines represent the change in the probability of giving up smoking between the ages of 33 and 42 for each additional adult learning course. The square line assumes that the relationship is linear, whereas the triangle line assumes that the relationship is non-linear.
Data source: 1958 National Child Development Survey

mid-adulthood, finding an effect was substantial. Feinstein and Hammond used four indicators of adult learning, courses taken leading to qualifications, courses taken not leading to qualifications, work-based learning and leisure courses. They found benefits for all four types of courses analysed, with the possible exception of vocational courses leading to accreditation. Academic courses appeared to be particularly important in relation to changing social and political attitudes, but taking leisure and work-related training courses had effects on a much broader range of outcomes than taking either vocational or academic courses leading to accreditation.

Further work on the area of adult learning made the link between childhood experiences of learning and childhood development to adult health outcomes and whether adult education could change earlier patterns (Hammond and Feinstein, 2006). The study demonstrated that those who participate in adult learning have positive transformations in wellbeing, optimism, efficacy (perceived control over important factors) and self-rated health. The magnitudes of the associations were not very large, but they were important nevertheless. The adjusted odds for transformed wellbeing were estimated to be between 1.2 and 1.3 times greater for those who took courses than they are for those who did not. Associations were not found between participation in adult learning and sustained or transformed satisfaction with life, depression, excessive drinking or obesity. What we highlight about these results is that adult learning can transform poor self-efficacy to good self-efficacy for those who were engaged in school but didn't get qualifications. It can also increase self-efficacy for those who were disengaged from school and left without qualifications. In conclusion, amongst those adults who did learning between the ages of 33 and 42 we observed substantial transformations in their health outcomes.

It is important to point out that the evidence presented so far does not prove that adult learning necessarily caused changes in health or civic participation. It could have been the case that other factors could have caused both adult education and positive changes in health and other social outcomes. However, people in this group who are having positive transformations in their lives were doing adult learning. They were more likely to have positive transformations if they did adult learning than if they did not. Hence, it might be that adult education is a safety ladder, a resource for life transformation, which is available to adults.

There is a big agenda for policy and research to understand the relationships between education trajectories, health trajectories, and employment trajectories in adult life, in order to provide better forms of learning for adults. And that there are potentially very high returns to investment in adult education as it could lead to reduced cost of ill-health and improved individuals' wellbeing.

Conclusions

In the preceding section, we described findings from three studies undertaken in the Centre, in which we tested the wider benefits of adult learning, finding that education had very important relationships with health. We have also investigated the relationship between the education of parents and their children's development (Feinstein, Duckworth and Sabates, 2004), education and social cohesion (Green, Preston and Sabates, 2003), participation in post compulsory schooling and engagement in crime (Feinstein and Sabates, 2005). In general, our findings suggest high returns to learning and the capacity of education to redress social class inequalities. However, in order to achieve this aim, education has to be provided in a way that does not exacerbate social class inequalities, in other words it has to achieve equality in access and quality provided.

In this concluding section, we try to explain why, despite substantial evidence that adult learning is very important for people's lives and that the skills people developed through wider forms of educational provision are key for a large number of social outcomes, there is not greater investment in adult education. What are the barriers to developing a broader model of lifelong learning that recognises that people need to go in and out of learning through-out their lives and need support for doing that? We set out five types of polit-ical and research barriers.

The first barrier is the narrow focus on human capital and a narrow concep-tualisation of economic threats to international economic competition. There is the sense that China and India represent huge competitive threats to the UK economy and therefore enhancing economic productivity, via improving the skills of the population, is central to maintaining our economic competi-tiveness. We believe that this is a narrow model of how economic competitive-ness is generated. There are important arguments over what forms of investment will best enable the UK to respond to these perceived productivity threats. Our research is based on the premise that a well functioning society, with high levels of equality, social engagement, civic participation and oppor-tunities for learning, will aid in sustaining good health and wellbeing to respond to the needs of new technologies. Simply increasing skills via the pro-vision of educational qualifications, without redressing social needs, will not be particularly productive in the long run. Our research suggests that social capi-tal, positive social networks and relationships between groups, high levels of social engagement, and personal resilience and mental health, are important for a well-functioning society that is going to be able to respond to the future challenges.

A second barrier has been around the notion that 'early is best'. There are good neuro-scientific bases for the view that early development is hugely important and that as a society we have underinvested in early years, and as a result recent investment in the early years has increased. Those in the adult learning sector need to develop a better response to this challenge, recognising the validity of the neuro-scientific evidence, but also putting it in the context of inter-generational transmission of success. A key element of the neurologi-cal development of the child in terms of the environmental input is cognitive stimulation and warmth in the home. These are provided by the parents, as well as by other important actors such as teachers, neighbours and other adults in the lives of children. Children learn best when they are taught by people who are also learning. So, the notion that in a very static sense early is best means that adult learning is not important is again a very narrow view that fails to recognise how we may actually input into the lives of children. In this sense, there is a double benefit to any investment in the learning of an adult, partic-ularly an adult who is also a parent or in other ways working with children. The call is for a better response to the 'early is best' notion and to understand the importance of intergenerational patterns.

The third barrier has been around the huge diversity of educational provi-sion that there is for adults. Adult learning is not a sector like other sectors in the sense that providers range widely in quality, mission and ethos. They are funded from different mechanisms and with various methods of account-ability. All of which make the adult learning sector very hard to study and eval-uate. We believe that there is relatively little knowledge about what is provided for whom, when, and what the effects are. Hence, to a certain extent, policy makers are working in the dark. The sector needs to make a better response and contribution in terms of data collection and analysis if it wants its benefits to be shown more widely.

A fourth difficulty is the separation of services for children and services for adults. Through Every Child Matters there has been a harmonisation and an integration of policy for children. Separately, there has also been some work on integrating adult services. But the breaking of the barrier between children's services and adult services continues to be a problem. The benefits of adult learning are broad and not experienced all in one government department so there is a separation between the funders of adult learning and those who get the benefits. In other words, the benefits of learning in terms of health may not be for the Department for Education (in whatever structural guise) but for the Department of Health, benefits of reducing crime may be beneficial for what was, until 2007, called the Home Office.

Because the benefits of learning are very broad and wide ranging, it has not been straightforward to focus government on provision more broadly, although the Department for Education and Skills developed a very effective focus on skill development, on achievement of Level 2 qualifications, on achievement of basic skills and increasingly on some vocational skills. However, this has not been within a framework which recognises the very important wider benefits of adult learning and particularly of learning that might be taken not for reasons of investment, not for narrow economic purposes, but maybe more of the manner of leisure, which is our final barrier. The contrast between learning as consumption for leisure, and learning as investment for economic returns, fails to recognise the very important reality that a healthy work/life balance is, in the long run, beneficial for individuals, families and communities. Learning has a very important role to play to achieve this aim. So, whether learning is considered as consumption or whether it is considered as investment needs much better conceptualisation than it has had up to recently.

References

Blundell, R., Dearden, L. and Meghir, C. (1996) *The determinants and effects of work related training in Britain*. London: The Institute for Fiscal Studies.

Brooks-Gunn, J. (1995) 'Children in families and communities: Risk and interventions in the bronfenbrenner tradition', in P. Moen, G.H. Elder and K.

Luescher (Eds.), *Examining Lives in Context. Perspectives on the Ecology of Human Development*. Washington, DC: American Psychological Association, pp. 467–519.

Chevalier, A. and Feinstein, L. (2006) 'Sheepskin or Prozac: The Causal Effect of Education on Mental Health', *Centre for Research on the Wider Benefits of Learning Discussion Paper*. London: Institute of Education.

Coleman, J. S. (1990). *The Foundations of Social Theory*. Cambridge, Massachusetts: Harvard University Press.

Feinstein, L. and Bynner, J. (2004) 'The importance of developmental trajectories in mid-childhood: Effects on adult outcomes in the UK 1970 Birth Cohort'. *Child Development*, 75(5), pp. 1329–1339.

Feinstein, L., Duckworth, K. and Sabates, R. (2004) 'A model of the inter-generational transmission of educational success', *Wider Benefits of Learning, Research Report 10*. London: Institute of Education.

Feinstein, L., Galindo-Rueda, F. and Vignoles, A. (2004) 'The labour market impact of adult education and training', *The Scottish Journal of Political Economy*, 51(2), pp. 266–280.

Feinstein, L. and Hammond, C. (2004) 'The contribution of adult learning to health and social capital', *Wider Benefits of Learning, Research Report No. 8*. London: Institute of Education.

Feinstein, L. and Sabates, R. (2005) 'Education and youth crime: effects of introducing the Education Maintenance Allowance programme', *Wider Benefits of Learning, Research Report 14*. London: Institute of Education.

Feinstein, L., Sabates, R., Anderson, T.M., Sorhaindo, A. and Hammond, C. (2006) *The effects of education on health: Concepts, evidence and policy implications*. Project Report, Centre for Innovation and Educational Research, OECD.

Green, A., Preston, J. and Sabates, R. (2003) 'Education, equity and social cohesion: a distributional model', *Wider Benefits of Learning, Research Report 7*. London: Institute of Education.

Grossman, M. (2005) 'Education and non-market outcomes', *NBER Working Paper 11582*. National Bureau of Economic Research, Cambridge MA.

Hammond, C. and Feinstein, L. (2006) 'Are those who flourished at school healthier adults? What role for adult education?', *Wider Benefits of Learning, Research Report 17*. London: Institute of Education.

Haveman, R. and Wolfe, B. (1984) 'Schooling and economic wellbeing: the role of non-market effects', *Journal of Human Resources,* 19(3): pp. 337–407.

Jenkins, A., Vignoles, A., Wolfe, A. and Galindo-Rueda, F. (2003) 'The determinants and labour market effects of lifelong learning', *Applied Economics*, 35, pp. 1711–1721.

Jenkins, A. (2006) 'Women, lifelong learning and transitions into employment', *Work, Employment and Society*, 20(2), pp. 306–328.

Lleras-Muney, A. (2005) 'The Relationship between Education and Adult Mortality in the United States', *Review of Economic Studies*, 72, pp. 189–221.

Luthar, S.S., Cicchetti, D. and Becker, B. (2000) 'The construct of resilience: a critical evaluaiton and guidelines for future work', *Child Development*, 71(3), pp. 543–562.

Markus, H. and Wurf, E. (1987) 'The dynamic self-concept', *Annual Review of Psychology*, 38, pp. 299–337.

Marsh, H.W. (1985) 'Age and sex effects in multiple dimensions of preadolescent self-concept', *Australian Journal of Psychology*, 37, pp. 197–204.

Marsh, H.W. (1990) 'A multidimensional, hierarchical model of self-concept: Theoretical and empirical justification', *Educational Psychology Review*, 2, pp. 77–172.

Putnam, R. (1995) 'Tuning In, Tuning Out: The Strange Disappearance of Social Capital in America', *PS: Political Sciences and Politics*, 27(4), pp. 664–667.

Schoon, I. and Bynner, J. (2003) 'Risk and resilience in the life course: Implications for interventions and social policies', *Journal of Youth Studies*, 6, pp. 21–31.

Shavelson, R.J. and Marsh, H. W. (1986) 'On the structure of self-concept', in R. Schwarzer (Ed), *Anxiety and Cognitions* Hillsdale, NJ: Erlbaum, pp. 305–330.

Spasojevic, J. (2003) *Effects of Education on Adult Health in Sweden: Results from a Natural Experiment.* New York: University of New York.

Thomas, C. and Morris, S. (2003) 'Cost of Depression among Adults in England in 2000', *British Journal of Psychiatry*, 183, pp. 514–519.

Weiss, A. (1995) 'Human capital vs. signalling explanations of wages', *Journal of Economic Perspectives*, 9(4): pp. 133–154.

CHAPTER 3

Adult literacy learning, participative democracy and the public collective good – new life for old causes?

URSULA HOWARD

Introduction

In this chapter I argue that in order to be relevant to the crucial social and global challenges we face, adult learning should not look back as much we do to the 'great tradition', whether by that we mean liberal adult education or the many social movements of the past, for guidance for the future. Instead we need to take what we need from the past to relate to what is happening now, and imagine our own future. We will need to be the inventors of new, responsive and flexible models that support the learning that communities, individuals and present-day already-established or nascent social movements want. In literacy, language and numeracy learning, for example, this approach would be based on the conception of literacy and learning as social practices, born of our need to communicate in the contexts in which we live and work, and help change for the better the situations in which people live.

Whilst adult learning can bring innovative energy and expertise to help people to change their lives, much current professional adult education follows policy or defends traditions not currently in favour. Thus it is focused on picking up the country's 'tail' of adult under-achievement, supporting the primary policy purpose of developing skills for the economy. These learners are typologised as dependent on state funding and subject to formal educative and curricular approaches which may not suit their purposes or motivations. The other aspect of efforts to keep adult learning as a policy concern is often focused more on defending state funding for adults' learning which is defined by educators rather than on the learning habits of people in the twenty-first century. Going to classes, including unaccredited ones, would be an expression of this type of provision. Ensuring funding for them from the state is a central focus for adult educators.

A more community-focused *Skills for Life* policy, for example, with social purpose matching the needs of individuals, would concentrate on inequality. Those people with the greatest learning needs, say at Entry 2 and below, and those with learning difficulties would be the highest priorities. They experience the greatest restrictions to their life chances; they have little imminent prospect of contributing to the economic agenda and in the current climate have not been prioritised. Within the drive for world-class skills, we must not neglect the civilising impetus of a democratic, community-based learning culture. And turning current logic on its head, we should count the economic cost of neglecting such large numbers of people living in poverty and unable, for many reasons, to develop and contribute their skills, real and potential.

The crisis of democracy and the role of adult learning

Currently, it can be argued, we are living with a low level of democracy. The representative democracy that permits a plurality of elites to represent the range of interests in society is perceived by many as narrow, restrictive and consequently a worryingly limited form of democracy. Decisions about profoundly important issues for ourselves, our children and grandchildren are taken by the executive, which appropriates and speaks and decides for an invented 'common sense' on fundamental issues such as war, terrorism, nuclear power, waste-disposal, parenting, gambling and drug-dependency, the social life of neighbourhoods and how to tackle literacy and numeracy problems.

Representative democracy often minimises the practice of social democracy, whereby people directly participate in the direction and government of their local communities. Consequently, for many people society – and to some extent even community – exist only at an increasingly abstract level. Private interests and the individual co-exist with the state: they have become aspects of each other. But they squeeze out any meaningful experience of society as a reality, or something a person belongs to, or is part of. Community, despite the relentless focus on individuals and families, remains a more meaningful, if conflicted reality – life and hope rests there, to be energised. Our planet is under grave threat from war, plunder and ecological meltdown. This is a crucial time to forestall further erosion of democracy and to set some limits to widening gulfs between rich and poor. It would benefit democracy and the survival chances of humankind if greater public understanding of the critical issues we face could be deepened, if the efforts people are making to address them could be conveyed, and opportunities for participation in action increased.

The contribution of adult learning

The history and some recent forms of literacy learning and practice – and adult learning more broadly – in the UK and across the world suggest that adult learning contributes to a healthier participative democracy and to social and community participation and activism (Feinstein and Hammond, 2004; Preston and Feinstein, 2004; 2005).

The greatest aspirational moments of adult learning, including those of the state, have been in rebuilding civil society, culture, respect and trust. An early example is the report of the Women's Employment Committee, the '1919 Report', on education in Britain which recognised women's educational needs in light of the social, academic and political changes following World War I (Ministry of Reconstruction, 1919). Perhaps the innovative energy of adult learning (especially literacy learning) should be most sharply focused on supporting learning: that is, learning which is already happening, potential or emergent, in civil society, in communities and in families. Professionals or 'organic intellectuals' could support rather than provide for the development of a wide variety of 'cultures', understood as 'ways of life' (Williams, 1961), and cultural expression; mindsets, strategies and actions would be less mesmerised by 'provision', 'delivery' and 'funding'. Reasserting adult education's historic links with big ideas like democracy, justice and equality is complex and challenging, as Martin (2006) has recently pointed out, given the tensions and conflicts of the present age. How much diversity can the 'public good' bear? One person's public good is another person's transgression, or worse. Putnam's (2006) latest work, for example, suggests that the greater the diversity in communities and neighbourhoods, the lower the levels of trust.

There is much evidence that the public value or long-term contribution to the public good and the development of mutual understanding across cultures made by adult education is immense. There are likely to be fewer examples of where the public good is better served than in developing the public's understanding of critical issues that affect their lives, and developing the capacity of individuals to participate more directly in the government of their local communities.

Building a new adult learning

Are we realistic in our often-voiced ambition for adult learning to reconnect to the social movements of the recent and distant past? What can we learn from the 1970s feminist, anti-poverty and literacy movements? The core issues have clearly not gone away (Thompson, 2007). What might we still learn from the adult learning which was organic to the social movements of the nineteenth century, ranging from literacy to astronomy and rhetoric? Perhaps the most potent but difficult pill to swallow is that more of the twentieth century models are not what we need. That would include state-led (local and national) adult education, perhaps best exemplified by the London County Council (LCC) between the two world wars; the Inner London Education Authority (ILEA) in the 1960s to early 1980s; the 1970s community and social movements, and the Greater London Council's popular planning initiatives. They are not the only answers. The timetabled, institutional classroom/learning-centre based model has so often failed to reach those with the greatest learning needs. It may work for pottery, art, and lecture series in a host of subjects and may work best for those already attuned to or successful in education, but it has worked less well for people who are under-achieving, including in language, literacy or numeracy. And it does not contribute a great deal any longer to creating a sense of society or community to which the majority can relate.

Should we not better focus our energies on inventing a new culture of adult learning to meet the challenges of social decline, the retreat into the private, climate change, hunger, religious/social differences, gross inequalities of wealth, endemic literacy and numeracy crises and a general poverty of ambition to create strong communities and re-create a sense of society and a louder public, collective voice about the key issues facing each and every one of us. Could the concept of the 'organic intellectual' Gramsci (1971), for one, be developed as a way of thinking afresh about the role of adult educators now? We should develop a new generation of people who could lead the development of adult learning for the future. Their role would be to act as both practitioners and creators of new models for formal and informal learning. They would help to enrich and extend the narrowly-focused skills-led approach to learning and the current focus of policy and professional practices on centralised curriculum models, simple lines of achievement and progression and individualised learning. As I write, in January 2008, the government is about to consult on a new model for informal, accredited learning and this may well be a unique opportunity for us to think radically and to create some exciting new traditions for adult learning.

We could be suggesting radically different, but practical, new models. We know from research into adult literacy in the US, for example, that people with very low levels of literacy skill still engage in self-study when they can't attend classes (Reder and Strawn, 2001). But the post-16 education system is not geared systematically to helping them. We have been talking about flexibility and 'open learning' since the 1980s, but have done very little about it, outside of 'project-based' schemes, pathfinders and pilots, usually with a limited funding span. They have not radically changed models of delivery. More radical forms of adult education could focus their efforts on discovering and supporting that which communities want, getting in behind communities as the mainstream way of establishing how and what learning happens, rather than featuring as the most interesting innovations around a traditional centre.

Learning and knowledge are contested areas, nowhere more so than in literacy, numeracy and language. In Shakespeare's *Henry VI* literacy was a sign of oppressive power and autocracy, distrusted by the people. For others it was emancipation. Brian Street's (1985) analysis of literacy as a social practice that differs significantly from society to society and, even among social classes within the same society, is critical to this scenario. Whose literacy is being learned? Is it the official 'autonomous' literacy (in language, 'standard' English, brilliantly counteracted by David Crystal's (2005) analysis of the historical development or stories of how varieties of English root themselves)? Or is it the literacy and language which are practised by people, the social practice model, or what Brian Street terms 'ideological' in contrast to 'autonomous'? Numeracy and maths learning and usages have cultural differences, too.

Skills for Life

England's current literacy drive, *Skills for Life*, is an example of 'autonomous' official literacy with a large apparatus for 'delivering' learning as a fairly prescribed set of skills and knowledge. It is symptomatic that writing (that is, composing text) is secondary; as is problem-solving in maths. And that the assessment regime is based on multiple choices, or reacting to text rather than creating it. Yet we know from research that practising literacy for your own or wider purposes supports the development of skills. And that literacy is a 'social practice' born of the need to communicate in writing – in communities. As Ivanič (2006) comments:

> *Taking a social perspective of language, literacy and numeracy involves paying attention first and foremost to the contexts, purposes and practices in which language, written language and numbers play a part.*

Yet classrooms routinely follow individualised learning schemes, symbolised by individual learning plans, often carried out in silent separation from other learners with little social interaction, despite robust evidence that effective learning and progress can be correlated with lively social interaction, talk and cooperation on ideas and tasks.

Where should adult educators stand on this? The *Skills for Life* strategy has offered massive funding and learning opportunities for millions. It has put 'disadvantaged adults' at the centre of policy. It has offered a model whereby the learners with the greatest needs are taught by fully-qualified, professional teachers. On the other hand, that learning is constrained in a top-down, government-directed model which leaves little room for independent, self-determined learning, collective or individual. And the demands of a numerical government target have resulted in drift, away from those with the greatest needs, to those who can most quickly cross thresholds. Level 2 is increasingly the focus, not Entry level.

The future is now and different

Adult learning can itself be a form of participatory democracy in which human connectivity grows organically through shared purposes. The current individualised models do not support that: teachers and adult learning advocates and professionals do need to feel empowered to push at the boundaries of the current model. Too much energy is sapped responding to policy and seeking to bend it to their values. There is little mental or emotional space for thinking anew in a radical or fundamental way. There is almost a sense that this would be self-indulgent, or an assumption that 'radical' equates to a return to the past.

Yet we must use the past to inform the future. Informal, self-generated learning in communities has worked before and could work again, supported by all the talents and experience which adult educators could bring to it. Here and now it seems urgent to break the silences, the utilitarian pragmatism and the inter-organisational competitiveness into which the pressures of work, policy imperatives and obsessions about funding drive us. We need to think afresh and find a bold voice to express what adult learning is all for.

What aspects of Freire's philosophy could we use today, drawing on his view of literacy as a form of cultural politics, emancipation and social equality? We need a political philosophy which can offer adult learning a critique and a way forward to address the concepts of 'social justice' and 'social mobility', used blandly as almost interchangeable terms and nearly always in the context of individual learning and life. Adult learning has a proud history of enabling independence also to mean interdependence, mutual understanding between people, communities and nations, expression of voice, resistance, opposition and positive development: for peace, against funding cuts, for popular planning and the resolution of local disputes. Has voluntary, informal adult learning retreated into, or moved forward into, civil society, individual choice, and corporate culture, leaving the state – and professional adult educators – to pick up the 'tail of under-achievement'(that is, focused and targeted adult skills learning) with basic skills at the heart of raising attainment and maintaining competitiveness? If so, this upholds social divisions. The kinds of learning eligible for funding attach to kinds of learners who are then typologised or stereotyped as 'dependent' on state funding, subject to approaches which may not suit their purposes or motivations.

Adult learning as it has been professionally practised has failed to contribute enough to a lessening of social divisions, which many of the movements within it or associated with it or supported by it have set out to do over two centuries and more. Old literacy as it was learned in eighteenth and nineteenth centuries – very successfully by many – was informally learned for self, family and community purposes, in self-taught, usually group settings. A 'new literacy', supporting people's purposes in the twenty-first century, could contribute to a more buoyant, more shared, less privatised civil society and a world in which people know enough about what to do to sustain it for their children and grandchildren.

A core part of the new literacy should be a focus on inequality. Again research shows the way. John Bynner and Sam Parsons (2006; 2007) have shown how desperately much greater is the inequality in life chances and life outcomes for people with literacy and numeracy skills at Entry 2 and below in the English literacy learning infrastructure. It is much greater than for those just one notch up at Entry 3, and counting towards the Public Service Agreement target. *Skills for Life* does not yet prioritise their needs, for example, by affording them the status of counting towards the target. The logic of the targets and the preoccupation with Level 2 skills to support competitiveness has left inequality parked by the wayside. There is interest; we need to ignite the political will to support learners who may need years to learn to Level 2, even if we know that learning makes a huge difference to them and to their employment prospects as well as to their health, happiness, personal attachment and civic participation.

The government's response to the Leitch report (2006), World Class Skills (2007) is now driving all before it. Policy, is poised to challenge the role of FE colleges, which have been a continuous presence in communities for over 160 years, offering stability, continuity and practical purpose to people, if not always inspiration for change. The threat to these organisations and their replacement with employer-based adult skills development is a move in the wrong direction for the re-kindling of a social and community spirit. It will also serve to diminish, not increase, the skills needed for the economy. This is because such narrow skills are not what employers want or need. As well as skills and knowledge, adult learning is about addressing inequality: social, financial and educational – and promoting health and happiness. Leitch himself talks about the need for a culture of learning and not ignoring those with learning difficulties. We have the knowledge to tackle these issues. Will we rise to the occasion and say inequality of this kind is not in the interests of the 'public good', or of society? What would such a movement look like? It needs to embrace the broader learning of good communication; a sense of other people; to know how to solve problems; to work with purpose and pride; to create ideas and imagine solutions; and to develop new skills which will help the UK. This is what a future adult learning policy and practice can generate. Thinkers, activists and professional educators are all needed to enable this new learning revolution to happen. And revolution it will need to be.

Conclusion

Adult learning can contribute to a more inclusive society with less inequality and a meaningful, shared understanding of and actions for the public good and a stronger participatory democracy. A major issue for adult educators is whether there should be more focus on skills, narrow or broad, rather than on 'seriously useful, (or useless) knowledge'. We are desperately in need of seriously useful knowledge and the skills for economic survival. Must this be at the expense of the knowledge, purpose and action which is needed literally to save the world? We also urgently need to fight for the space, among the clamour of voices, and the disaffection with the politics of the public, to find a moral and catching spirit to ignite new debates and a new sense of possibility for a democratic, learning culture.

References

Bynner, J. and Parsons, S. (2006) *New Light on Literacy and Numeracy*. London: NRDC.

Bynner, J. and Parsons, S. (forthcoming) *Illuminating Disadvantage*. London: NRDC.

Crystal, D. (2006) *How Language Works*. London: Penguin.

DIUS (2007) *World Class Skills: Implementing the Leitch Review of Skills in England*. London: DIUS.

Feinstein, L. and Hammond, C. (2004) 'The contribution of adult learning to health and social capital', *Wider Benefits of Learning, Research Report No. 8*. London: Institute of Education.

Freire, P. (1970) *Pedagogy of the Oppressed*. New York: Seabury.

Gramsci, A. (1971) *Selections From the Prison Notebooks*. London: Laurence and Wishart.

Ivanič, R., Appleby, Y., Hodge, R., Tusting, K. and Barton, D. (2006) *Linking Learning and Everyday Life: A Social Perspective on Adult Language, Literacy and Numeracy*. London: NRDC.

Leitch, S. (2006) *Leitch Review of Skills: Prosperity for All in the Global Economy – Final Report*. London: DIUS.

Martin, I. (2006) 'Where have all the flowers gone?', *Adults Learning* Vol. 18, No. 2. Leicester: NIACE.

Ministry of Reconstruction (1919) *Report of the Women's Employment Committee*. London: HMSO.

Paretsky, S. (2007) *Writing in an Age of Silence*. New York: Verso.

Preston, J.P. and Feinstein, L. (2004) 'Adult education and attitude change', *Wider Benefits of Learning*, Research Report No. 11. London: Institute of Education.

Preston, J., Feinstein, L. and Anderson, T.M. (2005) 'Can adult education change extremist attitudes?', *London Review of Education* 3(3): pp. 289-309.

Putnam, R.D. (2006) *Bowling Alone: The Collapse and Revival of American Community*. Tokyo: Kashiwashobo.

Reder, S. and Strawn, C. (2001) 'Program participation and self-directed learning to improve basic skills', *Focus on Basics*, Volume 4, Issue D. NCSALL.

Street, B. (1985) *Literacy in Theory and Practice*. Cambridge: Cambridge University Press.

Thompson, J. (2007) 'Time to use the "F" word again', in Tuckett, A. (ed) *Participation and the Pursuit of Equality: Essays in Adult Learning, Widening Participation and Achievements*. Leicester: NIACE.

Williams, R. (1961) *The Long Revolution*. London: Chatto and Windus.

CHAPTER 4

The right to make the wrong choices – liberty, learning and credit systems in the twenty-first century

CAROLE STOTT AND FINBAR LILLIS

Overview

This chapter considers the potential impact of the introduction of a credit system on the public value of learning and achievement into the future. Using existing research evidence it explores how credit could affect the way adults perceive learning and how society judges its value. How might the relationship change between individual achievement and the added social and economic benefits to society? A right to recognition of learning achievements (regardless of who pays), using credit as the currency, could in the future have a much wider impact than we realise on how we value and trade the outcomes of our learning.

What sort of 'credit' are we talking about? There are several 'credit frameworks' in the UK and there are credit systems in use in the US, NZ, Australia and Ireland and elsewhere. There is a great deal of interest in other countries looking to leapfrog the UK – and countries like ours – to put in place a system of qualifications which is more reflective of what their economies want and need. We are not (you will be happy to hear) exploring the nuances of different credit systems in this chapter. But we do need to explain what we mean by credit. So, in plain English:

- Credit is a means of valuing and recognising learning achievements.
- Credit gives a value to coherent sets of learning achievements at a designated level.
- These sets of achievements are organised into units which are assigned a level and an appropriate credit value. A unit may have a credit value of 1 credit at Level 2, for example. When all the specified achievements in a unit are achieved and verified a person can be awarded credit(s).

- **The three key components of a credit framework are therefore UNITS which have a CREDIT value and a LEVEL.**
- Credits can be combined and accumulated towards particular targets. These targets may include achievement of whole qualifications, each of which will specify the rules for achieving and combining credit to achieve that qualification.
- A person's achievements may include credits at different levels.
- Credit can be used to value and recognise all learning achievement.

Credit control: who will determine the value of the new currency of achievement?

Surely we should all have the right to make the wrong choices?

The credit idea has been around for a while and those who talked it up in the 1990s may think it is old news. But talk about credit was limited to the few and talk is somewhat different from making it happen. The economic and cultural landscape is not as it was in 1992. Early signs from the tests and trials of the Qualifications and Credit Framework (QCF)[1] suggest it may well have a far wider impact on learning and achievement than dreamed of by earlier theorists.

There are significant failures in the current qualifications system and this chapter explores some of those. However, policy reform tends rarely to look further than just around the corner. This chapter speculates on the impact of credit later in the twenty-first century. What would happen if the state gradually withdrew from central control of the qualifications system? Where qualification regulation shrinks and demand is all: where whatever public funding is available is directed at what the state wants (rather than by generalising what it does not); and employers and individuals dictate what counts.

What if credit became the currency of *achievement*, whether learning was publicly funded or not? What if qualification regulation were concerned only with maintaining the necessary quality and viability of the system and intervention were confined to balancing supply, demand and credit inflation – rather than determining the minutiae of supply? The trend suggests that the system is – over time – heading that way.

How, what and where we learn is changing fast. In this new market, how will we check the quality of the learning products we buy? Despite attempts to guarantee the quality of learning and qualifications, we know, for example, that much of it below Level 2 has, to date, been well below standard. There are no guarantees that education and training outside the publicly-funded system is any better – ask any major employer.

Perhaps as consumers of learning it is time we had consumer rights. In Europe, as public services are opened up to markets, this is what we expect – in order to protect the consumer from the market's worst excesses, maintain minimum standards and drive up the quality of products in the market.

Consumer rights must be universal and consumers include individuals, employers, non-governmental organisations and the State. And we know that those who don't pay have the least say and that their rights must be protected too. After all, the State in this new future will be a proxy consumer alongside others and should expect to get equal value for its investment.

Learning how to exercise such rights in the traditionally supply-driven world of education will become a key skill; and as consumers sharpen their learning skills and demands, providers must improve the way they address learner rights.

In a context where demand is driven by consumers, where credit is used to underwrite the value and currency of what we achieve (wherever and however we achieve it), and consumer rights are used to protect the consumer from being (completely) sold short, surely the logical trajectory of current reform is that the State steps back from defining and circumscribing what learning is of value.

And as learners and employers become more accustomed to paying for learning, surely they will only pay for what they want? Those of us with the cash already have that privilege when we shop for anything else in the market. But how do consumers ensure they get what they want without being sold short? We suggest that consumer rights should be expressed as universal entitlements. Learning the skills you need to *exercise* such rights in your own interest places a new responsibility on educators in the system, and educators will have a particular responsibility to inculcate such skills among those with the least influence in the market.

The State and the education system have always given us what it thinks we need. But as the system changes and demand instead of supply begins to dominate, we should all be sufficiently informed to exercise the right to make the wrong choices.

Public value and adult learning

We take 'public value' to mean any perceived additional beneficial value to wider society that accrues from individual participation in (adult) learning. This additional public value is variously associated with improved public health, better personal and community relationships, a more 'inclusive' society and improved prospects for wealth and prosperity. Participation in adult learning is meant to accrue such benefits to wider society. Of course there are different views as to what constitutes 'public value': learning should liberate our society from ignorance, perhaps; or learning should improve our skills and competitiveness, thus releasing us all from poverty and bringing benefits to the poor as well as the rich – the tide which lifts all boats. . .

We assume in this chapter that the public value of adult learning can embrace both the quest for social justice and the demands of a globalised economy. There is the well-known tension between the two, and credit has the potential to help deliver either or both of these benefits. We argue that credit will open up what and how we learn, and how we recognise and value what we achieve. Credit has the potential to liberate us from the constraints of the current qualification system – whether for societal good or ill depends upon your perspective of the public value of adult learning, what you consider to be the wider social purpose of investing in adult learning.

The quest for social justice

Our understanding of social justice reflects the core principles described by David Miller.[2] Miller argues that the core idea of social justice is contained in the following principles:

- equal citizenship – concerned with how we enjoy and exercise equal civil and political rights;
- the social minimum – concerned with what people must have to live a decent life in society;
- equality of opportunity – that a person's life chances should depend on their abilities and motivation (including everyone having a fair chance to acquire skills and abilities); and
- fair distribution – that distribution of goods and resources beyond the demands of equal citizenship and the social minimum should be fair.

Social justice is not simply about the distribution of resources and opportunities, and nor is it about just improving individual welfare. Fundamentally it's concerned with living together in a fair society and the responsibilities and rights that go with that.

As society constantly changes and develops so achieving social justice is a continuous quest. The threats to our planet and advances in medicine and technology create new rights and new responsibilities and we have constantly to assess what social justice means in these contexts.

Nor does social justice result solely from government policy. It depends critically on how each of us behaves; how we exercise our responsibilities and assert our rights, including our right and responsibility to influence government.

The demands of a global economy

The economic arguments for skills development are cogently made elsewhere in this book. Chris Humphries' chapter sets out the case for skills reform.[3] He also says that economic development and social cohesion are two sides of the same coin: that in order to be truly competitive, society needs to create opportunities for all to achieve their potential and the benefits of a strong economy need to be enjoyed by all its citizens.

The challenges and the imperatives for improved adult skills to sustain and develop our economic competitiveness are clearly set out in Chris' chapter.

Protectionism and the qualifications system

If we are to meet these challenges for social justice and economic competitiveness then protectionism, where vested interests and those who currently gain most benefit seek to maintain the *status quo*, cannot be tolerated. Protectionism should be challenged by progressive societies. It is perhaps one of the biggest threats to social justice and to global economic prosperity and opportunity. Protectionism manifests itself at all levels and in all spheres, in global businesses, in public and political institutions, in local communities and in the qualifications system.

Our qualifications system too often appears to protect the interests of a few at the expense of the least able and the least economically powerful in our society. Implementation of the current reform programme has been a struggle against those who seek to protect their own interests (institutional, economic and cultural) and who work hard to maintain the *status quo*. The current struggle to keep the credit system under their control – is actually to limit its potential so as to maintain what we have. This is done often in the name of quality, coherence and robustness – legitimate arguments were they not (when you scrape away at the surface) almost always much more subjective in detail than they sound.

The failure of the current system – learning and valuing achievement

How good is the current system at helping people to learn and get recognition for what they achieve?

It is easy to find evidence that our current system is a weak foundation for achieving either social justice or economic competitiveness. OECD data confirms that the UK lags behind in labour productivity and has a large proportion of low-skilled adults (the UK is ranked in the lower half of OECD countries). In 2004, 30 per cent of adults of working age did not hold qualifications at Level 2. Countless research reports show the continued link between low social class and low achievement.[4] To quote Helena Kennedy, 'if at first you don't succeed you don't succeed'. The failure of the compulsory school system to equip 49 per cent of our 16-year-olds with a Level 2 qualification (five GCSEs or equivalent) is well documented. This inequality and failure throughout our system has been a constant feature for over a century.

It seems that from secondary school onwards we fail to get the foundations of the system right. It is relatively recently that adult basic literacy and numeracy has received public attention with resources and a strategy to match. It was only in March 2006 that the White Paper finally recognised the need to bring coherence and resources to the development of a Foundation Learning Tier.

Prior to that, ministers and others in public life had made reference to the failure of the system below Level 2 (in reference to our poor skills performance at that level) but there had been little research to examine why the existing system had failed to support adults to achieve and progress.

The failure of the current system for adults without qualifications

Credit Works conducted research for the Learning and Skills Council (LSC) in 2006 into the market failure of curriculum and qualifications below Level 2.[5] We examined current research, reviewed data and information about learning and achievement, conducted interviews with 27 policy-makers and providers and 47 learners. Frankly, we found a depressing picture of adult learning below Level 2.

We found, in summary:

- an emphasis within the system on courses and participation, not always matched by an equal emphasis on priority learners and progression;
- insufficient development and use of more sophisticated market intelligence to analyse the needs and motivators of different groups within the broader group of people who are socially excluded and/or do not have qualifications at Level 2;
- insufficient development and use of more sophisticated individual needs analysis and ongoing monitoring and review;
- a failure to develop and design qualifications and curricula below Level 2 with the needs of priority groups paramount;
- insufficient flexibility in qualification and curriculum structures to promote and support progression;
- a lack of consistent ongoing learner advice and support for adults;
- a systematic failure to map and monitor routes, pathways and destinations for learners;

- a failure to develop and manage partnership arrangements which will effectively support the engagement and progression of priority learners; and
- lack of an overall strategy to build capacity across the system to support learning and progression for priority learners below Level 2.

So for those who do not succeed at school the prospect of succeeding as adult learners is stunningly unlikely. In 2002 it took a participating adult without a Level 2 qualification *14 years* on average to get one. So for those of us who like to think that adult learning as it stands needs protecting (either from those soft liberals who would spend public money willy-nilly on pink and fluffy useless stuff, or from the target-driven suits who would reduce all adult achievement to any old Level 2 NVQ) there is a stark message: as it stands the system does not deliver either way. Very, very few (3 per cent) of adults without Level 2 qualifications participate at all – and a tiny proportion of them progress – however you define progression.

The flaws outlined are not present in just one part of the system; they are almost universal and often interrelated – and not just down to providers. They are inherent in a system heavily driven by qualifications which are rarely fit for purpose for those without them.

Those who don't pay have the least say: creating a manifesto for learner rights in the Foundation Learning Tier

Consumer rights, especially for those with the least say

The Foundation Learning Tier (FLT) is part of the Government's response to this market failure. After conducting a substantial volume of research for the LSC and Qualifications and Curriculum Authority (QCA) in recent years we began (as you might expect) to see a pattern in the issues faced: in the struggles of Entry to Employment (E2E) providers with the qualifications system; in the absence of understanding and use of Accreditation of Prior Learning (APL); in first steps learning being characterised as a funding stream rather than a learning experience; and in recommendations from Credit Works research reports[6] which coalesced in a proposed set of 'entitlements' or consumer rights for learners in the FLT.

These rights were designed to create upward pressure on reform of the system. 'Learner entitlement' has up to now marked out those that could have free or supported access to a (circumscribed) offer of publicly-funded learning. Whether or not the free offer was what they wanted or was any good was another matter.

We hoped this could change as the FLT tested a different concept of entitlement for adult learners and established the principle across all education of consumer rights (regardless of who pays):

"By 2010 all learners without Level 2 qualifications will be entitled to:

- **Personalised learning** as follows:
  - **Personalised choice** – which will include using credit-based units to design and compose programmes and qualifications which enable learners to pursue validated progression pathways through the FLT (within a credit and qualifications framework as it develops and is implemented) according to their abilities and interests.
  - **A personalised learning experience** – which means personalising the experience of learning; so that an individual experiences learning and achievement in a way which suits their preferred learning styles, promotes personal ownership, autonomy and control of their learning and achievement.
  - **Recognition of achievement** and access to progression pathways from the outset of their learning journey in the FLT. All achievements will have currency and validity and have the potential to count towards qualifications in the qualifications and credit framework.
  - **Access to a coherent curriculum** which develops and integrates functional literacy and numeracy; personal and social development learning which 'unblocks' obstacles to progression; vocational and subject learning which provides skills and knowledge for employability."[7]

So, by 2010 all learners without Level 2 qualifications should be entitled to have their achievements recognised in the Qualifications and Credit Framework (QCF) including those informal achievements acquired right from the outset of the learner's journey; they should be entitled to personalised learning which reflects their interests, abilities and choices; and entitled to a coherent and progressive learning experience – one which leads somewhere the learner needs to go (rather than where the provider wants to drop them off).

With the tests and trials of the QCF we are at last testing a system which offers the potential to create a subtle profile of learners' achievements over time, which will redefine qualifications quite differently from the awkward offers we have now and which will – when learners get the hang of it – lead to new and different demands being made on providers and the systems that providers have to deal with. Achievements in the FLT will count in one step towards qualifications in the QCF – no more preparing learners to be ready for qualifications sometime next year, sometime never.

Given the Delphic value attributed to OECD performance tables and Leitch's[8] aspiration to keep the UK somewhere in the OECD top quartile, the position of qualifications as a success measure looks pretty well assured. But the QCF offers the chance for learners and employers to exert more influence on the content and design of qualifications – redefining what is of value – a more subtle appreciation of what constitutes successful achievement in the FLT (and at Levels 2 and 3) and a better match to demand.

Adult learners will need skills and confidence to gain control of their own learning and achievement and to begin to demand what they need instead of taking what they are given. Those who don't pay have the least say – so making these new entitlements work in the FLT will be a real test of how far the system really wants learners to exercise such rights. There will be the question of how much the state and professionals are prepared to trust the public to determine which learning achievements are valued.

Implications for providers

And there are of course consequences for providers in equipping learners with the right skills, inculcating the right attitudes, changing how we use IAG (Information, Advice and Guidance) and the ongoing review of learner progress. Most of all, providers need to know that reform of the system will enable them to deliver what learners want and need, that the right products are out there and that the focus of public funding is sharp enough to recognise which learner is entitled to support from public funds – and which acknowledges that clumsy categorisation and cross-matching of adult learners, provision and qualifications is not enough.

The prize is the creation of a different dynamic between learners and providers and the system which underpins that relationship – and the recent FE Bill[9] could put learner influence on FE into law for the first time. A real voice and influence for learners introduces a new force for change in the system, one which has the power to work with policy reform from the top to squeeze reform from the bottom up.

Learners could at last be given some leverage in the system, alongside that now being extended to employers. Giving learners the means to exert some direct influence will challenge embedded vested interests and help maintain momentum of reform towards a "demand-led" system through successive administrations and changes in the learning and skills landscape.

The impact and influence on reform of introducing these entitlements could outlast the efforts of any single government.

Recognition of achievement: entitlement to credit and progression

Of course each of the entitlements we describe is interrelated and interdependent. But we want to focus on one – that all learners should be entitled to and have access to, recognition of learning achievements and to progression. We want to extrapolate and take the concept of entitlement to recognition of achievement forward into uncharted territory, beyond the system as it now stands and beyond the use of credit to simply disaggregate existing conventional qualifications.

Does accreditation skew the learning experience?

Whether or not people want access to recognition of achievement has exercised those working in the field of adult learning for many years and perhaps quite rightly so. The danger that accreditation will skew and/or homogenise the learning experience is a real one.

Do adult learners get a choice?

Adult learners often find themselves on 'accredited' or 'non-accredited' courses – that is, programmes which do or do not lead to external recognition of achievement. They may or may not have made a choice for or against accreditation. Usually the chosen course is accredited or not, irrespective of any learner preference. The choice to opt in to accreditation and gain formal recognition at a chosen point along a learning journey does not exist in practice.

Qualifications and curriculum – the tail wagging the dog

One major reason is that qualifications drive the curriculum – the tail wags the dog. Qualifications are pre-written achievement sets which tightly circumscribe what the individual has to learn to achieve them. Exactly how they learn may well be driven by prescribed assessment requirements. There may be sensible reasons for prescription – to meet licence-to-practise requirements, for example, for the sake of public safety. There is, we know, some flexibility in modern qualifications but the scope for recognising individual achievements is still rare. Increasing the flexibility of qualifications has often been resisted – because of a worry that opportunities for recognition of 'partial achievement' might dissuade learners and employers from pursuing 'whole' qualifications. Assessment has to be 'robust' and reliable – and is often prescribed in the interests of ensuring valid and consistent results – though not necessarily with the preferences of learners and employers, or the reality of learning in the workplace, in mind.

The academy expects

Achievement and the acquisition of knowledge have to be underwritten by 'the academy' of institutional educational interest. This presents a big obstacle to reform. Even when we consider learning and achievement at Entry levels and Level 1, the influence of the academy on appropriate assessment, the need for completion of 'whole qualifications' remains influential, even where those achieving such qualifications are unlikely to progress to university. The need for robust systems of assessment in 'vocational' education is driven by the need to match the apparent robustness of assessment in academic qualifications.[10] How far any of these requirements assist in bringing the achievement of skills to the unqualified or access to social justice is, at best, questionable.

The limited purposes of qualifications

Qualifications do not currently have a wide range of purposes. Only a limited number signify a licence-to-practise. For the majority, once achieved they are used as a means of entry to another level of study, an institution or the work-place. Employers have low expectations of the State qualifications system.[11] They believe that qualifications either equip young people or adults with 'the basics' or are a means of entry to university. Beyond this they are sceptical about the value of vocational qualifications not acquired in the workplace, and prefer when spending their own money to spend it on learning which is tailored to their needs: *they often don't want to pay for the whole NVQ – they don't need it*, as one sector representative said in a recent interview.[12]

A right to recognition: the consequences of making credit an entitlement

Do learners want recognition of achievement?

Almost all the adult learners we interviewed in two recent studies wanted access to recognition of achievement and understood how credit could be used to build up a profile or a qualification over time, *like pieces of a cake*, as one learner put it.

Their demand for credit was conditional, however, and their conditions seem reasonable enough: that they should be able to opt in to accreditation as and when they are ready for it; that accreditation should reflect their learning and not drive it; that the assessments and evidence should be meaningful to them as learners; and that credit should help you to progress to the job you want, or to another programme of learning. What you learn and achieve should count towards a national qualification in one step and you should not always have to go back to the beginning every time you start a new programme or change direction.

These views helped to shape the details of the manifesto for learners outlined above and present a huge challenge to the qualifications system and all those who are driven by it (willingly or not).

Using credit to reform the experience of learning and achievement –
letting learners and employers choose

It is possible to develop a genuinely responsive and flexible system of recognition and qualification using credit, and this is ostensibly the goal of the QCF. However, it is also possible to create a credit framework and then make attempts to preclude choice by creating inflexible rules of combination. We are not suggesting that this is happening now, though there will be interests that seek to maintain the same level of prescription in designing new credit-based qualifications that exist in current conventional ones.

However, we think (perhaps optimistically, but we shall see) that once the credit genie is out of the bottle it may be difficult to get it back in again. Time after time in interviews with employers, learners and providers we have found a ready understanding of the potential of a credit system to at last give employers what they want, to allow providers to design programmes that meet different demands and which could allow learners to take, own and transfer (or even trade) their achievements in ways which they cannot do now. Creating a credit framework and attempting to prescribe how it is used is like designing a park with one path through it. People will sooner or later stray from the path and new pathways will wear down the turf and criss-cross the grass. Perhaps even the original path designed by committee will become overgrown.

Giving people a right to recognition for their achievements through credit can create a positive view of recognition. It can create a different relationship between the producers and the users of qualifications. Currently qualifications are designed and produced by the system (awarding bodies, sector bodies and regulators all play a role). Learners are little more than consumers of the products. An entitlement to credit, in a context of focusing on learner autonomy and personalisation with guidance and support, leads to a need for a dialogue where the value of learning is a negotiated and collaborative process between the public and the professionals.

This could result in a change over time in determining which skills are valued. For example, having the skills to manage your own learning, regulate your own behaviour, and "know what to do when you don't know what to do" could all become more valuable in a learning model founded on self-determination and autonomy. Currently these so-called soft skills carry little or no formal recognition or value. However, in a system where learners are entitled to credit, the learners gain a voice and influence; and the value of these skills to individuals, employers and society generally becomes determined by the relationship and process of dialogue and negotiation.

The right to recognition of achievements requires, at a minimum, that learning providers organise themselves to enable evidence of achievement to be gathered which can count towards the award of credit.

Using credit to promote the public value of adult learning

As well as excluding 30 per cent of our citizens, qualifications are a blunt instrument for measuring the skills and achievements of the population. We know that 30 per cent of adults do not have Level 2 qualifications, but we know little about what skills they *do* have. In truth we understand that placing any of us at a single level of skills acquisition may be convenient for statisticians but it is a poor reflection of reality.

Over time, credit can provide a much more subtle and sophisticated picture of UK PLC than our current qualifications. Instead of adding endless stars or grades to a single-level qualification – or worse, ignoring achievements because they are not 'complete' – we can reflect reality much more clearly.

Why, for example, does an A-Level have to be solely at Level 3? We know in practice some learners will produce achievements at Level 4, and at Level 2 in completing an A-Level. Why not have additional credit-based units at Level 4 which lead to credit exemption in higher level study? Why not include some units at Level 2 in an A-Level?

This is important for individuals as well as society. In the same way governments use data on skills levels to plan their improvement strategies, so individuals could plan and manage their learning in the same way. Of course many with high-level qualifications already work the existing system in this way and to their advantage. But there's little or no scope for doing this at lower levels or with any degree of precision or flexibility.

Attempts have been made to tackle this through Accreditation of Prior Learning (APL). Processes of APL, however, have become dominated by the demand for robust assessment. Learners' and employers' access to and understanding of such processes then requires 'expert' intermediaries to make them work, and outcomes of the whole experience are disproportionate to the effort and cost. It is, however, possible to integrate recognition of prior learning into the curriculum and actively accredit that prior learning within a learning programme.[13] Such a model should be meaningful as well as workable and there is always likely to be a need for this. But better still is a system where learners are *entitled* to credit for their achievements and providers obliged to organise themselves to provide evidence to demonstrate achievements from the outset.

Employers' views

Our research indicates that employers' expectations of the public qualifications system are largely concerned with how well the existing system prepares young people for work or higher education. There are, however, other acknowledged internal learning and development issues faced by employers, and traditionally employers would not look to or expect the qualifications system to help them address these. This may change (or be changing) with the introduction of new initiative such as Train to Gain and skills academies. However, the Confederation of British Industry suggests that a credit system could result in a more "user-led than supplier-led system" and welcomes this. There is evidence also that credit can support employee development; that given the chance employees will opt for credit; and that credit brings people back into learning at work and aids progression.[14]

Direct influence over what learning is considered to be of public value

There is evidence that credit is good for individuals, for business and the economy and can support social justice by enabling more people to gain the credentials and confidence to participate as equal citizens. Inevitably there are interests which will seek to continue to control and direct the qualification system.

Could entitlement and hence demand for credit for achievements result in a more participatory, negotiated and shared understanding of value and purpose? Could consumer rights introduce a different dynamic in the process of reform, giving more influence to the public in negotiating learning activities and outcomes? Will such influence alter what we consider to be of public value in adult learning?

Freedom to choose: the potential consequences

The right to make the wrong choice What would be the impact of allowing people real freedom of choice? There is certainly an argument that prescription in qualification design protects people from making uninformed choices and wasting their opportunities (and government resources). State-led or academy-led qualification design is then a protection against vulnerability to uninformed consumerism. But given the failure of the qualification system, especially at lower levels, would handing over choice to consumers really present a threat, given the current waste in our system?

Selfish acquisition versus the public good What is the relationship between entitlement, personal aspirations and selfish acquisition (the consumption of learning as a commodity)? How does that square with our liberal views on learning as a force for good? How does it relate to public value? Is entitlement more likely to lead to selfish consumerism than public value? How does entitlement to credit fit in with our model of public value, partnership and co-production?

Impact on standards What would be the impact of learners exercising entitlement to credit on our perceptions of standards? The number of people achieving GCSEs and A-Levels has rocketed and each year we see the annual backlash and accusations of lowering standards. How much of this is about standards of achievement and how much is about the function of traditional qualifications to select and protect an elite: where value is accorded in proportion to rarity? Surely any form of learning achievement can be recognised and quality assured, so is this really about standards?

Credit could see a massive increase in achievements. (Imagine if all the people achieving Microsoft qualifications, to take just one example, were getting credit recognised and valued in the public system.)

The adult educator and the learner If learners begin to exercise an entitlement to credit how will the relationship between the adult educator and the learner change? Are we professionals in the system going to feel uncomfortable with learners exercising their rights if it means we are losing control over what learners choose to learn?

It is difficult for individuals to manipulate the current qualification system (difficult for employers too). But what would be the consequences of professionals/producers losing control and direction? How (and can) we adapt our role as adult educators to a different model of creating and supporting what learning is of value?

Can the learner be trusted? Ultimately this may be a question of how much the State and vested interests are prepared to trust the public to take a real and active role in determining which achievements are valued. New models of governance and partnership are now being developed in public life: isn't it time we applied these same principles to qualifications? Quality assurance is a separate issue and process (although it is often used as a guise for control of content under the banner of maintaining standards). Dare we let the genie out of the bottle: give people an entitlement to credit; allow them a more prominent role in determining which skills are valued; relax the endless qualification rules except where they're genuinely essential; trust people to make the right choices and give them the freedom not to?

And as learners begin to pay more for their learning, how can an entitlement to credit possibly be refused?

Can we trust that, given choice and some control, in dialogue with the professionals, people will actively support serious learning which is of value to them and their communities?

Notes

1 This is the Qualifications and Credit Framework proposed for England, Wales and Northern Ireland (EWNI). The QCF is not just about sticking numbers on tired old qualifications or even on shiny new ones – it is about changing our perception of the notion of qualification itself.
2 Miller, D. (2005) 'What is Social Justice?', in *Social Justice, Building a Fairer Britain*. London: IPPR.
3 Humphries, C. (2006) *Skills in a Global Economy*. London: City & Guilds.
4 (See for example, Feinstein.)
5 Credit Works (2006) *Adult Learning, Skills and Progression to Level 2; A Study of Market Failure*. LSC.
6 Credit Works reports referenced throughout (2006).
7 LSC requirements for providers engaged in trials of the FLT.
8 Leitch Review of skills (2006) Prosperity for all in the Global Economy: World Class Skills. London: HM Treasury.
9 DfES. (2006) *Further Education and Training Bill*. London:DfES.
10 Torrance *et al.* 2005.
11 Credit Works (2005) *Key Issues in Including Employer-led Provision Currently Outside the NQF Within the Framework for Achievement*, QCA.
12 Credit Works (2006) publication for QCA, November – TBA.
13 Credit Works (2006) *The Feasibility of Employing the Accreditation of Prior Learning (APL) to Support Progress Towards the Achievement of Full Level 1, 2 and 3 Qualifications*. LSC June.
14 Credit Works (2005) *Key Issues in Including Employer-led Provision Currently Outside the NQF Within the Framework for Achievement*. QCA.

CHAPTER 5

Demonstrating public value

JOHN STONE

If the public sector reform agenda has run into trouble it can hardly be ascribed to a lack of government concern or a history of neglect. This is a Government which genuinely cares about public services and has smothered them with resources and initiatives since first coming into office in 1997. Ten years on, however, the aim of achieving a balance between the perceived quality of public services and public expectations remains as elusive as ever.

The further education system is not exempt, with the colleges being one of the key concerns highlighted by Sir Andrew Foster in his recent review. 'Colleges,' he asserted, 'should be enjoying a golden age, given the correspondence between their potential and the nation's needs. Colleges have an important role to play in delivering key Government priorities and strategies, yet they are hampered by their reputation and profile.'

Further education might be forgiven for feeling slightly frustrated by this characterisation. After all, the FE system has succeeded in meeting or exceeding most, if not all, of the key targets which have been set for it in recent years. Success rates continue to climb. Inspection grades improve and student satisfaction rates are amongst the highest in the public sector. So why is there still a problem?

It is perhaps cold comfort to colleges that they are not alone. Most of the public sector appears to be continually cast in a similar vein. This was highlighted by Tony Blair in his 6 June 2006 speech on public service reform. The warning, 'If we cannot show that the service has got radically better then consent from the public is in jeopardy', was widely reported. Justifiably so, as one might have expected a Prime Minister, at that stage in his administration, to be talking up the positive benefits which could be seen to flow from the increased funding enjoyed by the public sector over the past decade. Yet across the public sector, targets have been set and in many cases met, but still that elusive 'public service feel-good factor' fails to take hold.

This apparent failure to develop a model for securing acceptable levels of quality in public services follows several decades of high-profile development and experimentation. Back in the late 1980s it seemed very clear where the path to quality lay. Quality gurus such as Deming and Juran, who had initially been influential in Japanese engineering and manufacturing, found themselves reinterpreted for life in the service sector as the doctrine of Total Quality Management (TQM) took hold.

Early models focused on customers, and the clear role of a product or service was to meet or exceed their expectations. The TQM movement became associated with management models which placed great emphasis on frontline staff. Those deemed closest to their customers were to be 'empowered' and expected to get things 'right first time'. In this model, inspection became unnecessary or even counter-productive. Commentators compared the relative success of manufacturing companies such as Toyota, who adopted these principles, against less enlightened outfits who reputedly spent more time fixing the faults identified through the inspection process than Toyota did to build a car in the first place.

The strategies which evolved at that time were based on devolution and customer choice, with quality improvement driven externally by market demand and internally by self-assessment. These concepts are very much back on the agenda, but what is to be different this time around? As this approach failed to take hold in the past, are there lessons to be learned from the experience?

In reality the model adopted in learning and skills had always been something of a compromise. The 1992 Further and Higher Education Act brought us independent, incorporated colleges and a funding mechanism which followed the student. Students were, theoretically at least, empowered to exercise their choice in a free 'demand-led' market.

Inspection, however, as a mechanism to secure public accountability was retained, albeit initially to validate the self-assessment process.

The strengths of the model were soon apparent and growth, innovation and financial efficiency were delivered in spades. By the late 1990s, however, the system had begun to run into problems. There were a few high-profile failures and, by the measures of the time, the quality of outcomes was variable. The feeling grew that light-touch inspection allied to market power wielded through the free exercise of student choice provided an inadequate basis from which quality could be assured. The power relationship between the student and the institution, it could be argued, is so one-sided that students may not be sufficiently assertive to exercise their consumer rights. Many institutions operated effective local monopolies, further weakening the effectiveness of the market to self-regulate. Crucially, the New Labour Government was less certain than its predecessor over the ability of market mechanisms to widen participation and provide increased opportunities for the disadvantaged.

Levels of funding were also a major issue and the expectation of better funding for public services played a significant role in the election of the new Labour Government in 1997. After a slow start engineered by the 'prudent' election commitment to abide by the previous administration's spending plans, the Chancellor gradually let the brakes off public funding and the money began to flow.

Mindful, even then, of such largesse flowing down a large black hole, the phrase 'something for something' was on every minister's lips and, piece by piece, the models and metrics thought necessary to deliver this were gradually assembled.

Interestingly this approach was never spelt out in detail and it may never even have been planned as such, but in retrospect the key elements have become clear:

- the separation of responsibility for strategy from delivery and the creation of new strategic agencies to give a 'strategic' lead;
- the centralisation of planning functions either with Government, the new strategic bodies or, as often as not, somewhere in between;
- a high-profile regime of targets linked the national public sector agreements emanating from the Treasury; and
- a strengthened external accountability structure of inspection, performance metrics and sanctions.

The cumulative impact of this has been to shift the balance of strategic decision-making across the public services away from institutions in favour of central government and its agencies. Government will see this as the correct application of their democratic mandate providing greater powers for central planning, prioritisation of 'scarce' resources and the ability to intervene as and when circumstances require (for example, when an institution is failing to deliver adequately).

The model represents a fundamental break with the policy direction in place pre-1997 which tended to restrict national agencies to funding, leaving responsibility for quality and strategy with the delivery agencies themselves, in theory at least responding directly to the demands of their 'customers'.

In further education, the change in approach crystallised in the Learning and Skills Act 2000 and the creation of the Learning and Skills Council which, despite the inclusion of a complex sub-regional network, primarily provided the mechanisms for delivering a more centrally-directed system of national targets. Inspection was toughened up and, perhaps unsurprisingly, large numbers of colleges failed it, particularly in the first year, heightening concerns over the number of 'failing colleges'. Recruitment targets which reflected broad national priorities were set and attention focused on success rates as a key indicator of quality.

Since then there have been real achievements. Failing colleges have all but been eliminated (to have their place in the stocks taken by 'coasting colleges') and success rates have gone through the roof. But still concerns over public perception, underlying quality and responsiveness continue to drive the reform agenda. The situation is not so different in many other high-profile public services.

There is increasing concern that part of the problem, at least, lies with the model itself. Government ministers, notably David Milliband, exploring ideas such as 'double devolution', float alternatives. The air is once again thick with the language of the market place: 'demand-led', 'contestability', 'bureaucracy-busting', 'downsizing' and so on, but the impression persists that in Kuhnian terms the revolutionary move from one paradigm to the next has not yet occurred. We are largely dealing with problems apparent in the existing model, power is being eroded not relinquished, and the shape and dimension of a new paradigm has yet to emerge.

The inherent problems are, however, becoming clearer and derive from the following impediments faced by anyone trying to construct a rational deduction from the facts in any complex system:

- you can't get all the information;
- if you could you can't process it;
- you can't predict the future; and
- even if you could, things change.

In the real world there are quite simply too many potential ways in which any given system can be described or influenced. Paul Ormerod in *Why Most Things Fail*[1] describes this as 'the curse of dimensionality'. Even in something as constrained and rule-based as a game of chess the consequences of any given move on the development of the game will be largely unpredictable. In the real world the potential consequences of a series of actions multiply. Markets fall, policies fail, companies fail, and no satisfactory model exists to explain why or predict where the next failure will occur.

Policy-making also suffers from a fundamental (if sometimes deliberate) confusion between supporting evidence and proof. It is nearly always possible to unearth evidence to support any particular point of view but that does not, of course, prove that it is true or the best possible model available.

Decision-makers will take a view based on the facts as they see them, but the model they promote can only be an incomplete description of reality. As they cannot predict how a given situation will develop, it is not possible to predict with any certainty precisely what action one should take to achieve the desired result.

A rigid target-based accountability structure freezes in and magnifies the impact of an imperfect strategy making it impossible for the system to adapt in the light of developing circumstances.

The view continues to grow that perhaps target-setting itself, originally introduced to provide focus and accountability, has become part of the problem. It was legitimate for the Government to set out clear goals and priorities for its administration. The problems begin, however, when the approach is cascaded down the system to the extent that inappropriate management models are adopted at institutional and individual level.

Government and its strategic agencies cross the line between providing policy frameworks – which coordinate the direction of travel and influence priorities while still allowing the room for manoeuvre that agencies need to adapt to unforeseen local complexities – and imposing policy levers which effectively dictate decision-making on the ground.

In any normal enterprise there is a constant interplay between strategy and operations and continual adjustments are made by management and staff to reflect and adapt to the unpredictable impact of real world events. This has been described as more akin to 'white-water rafting than steering an ocean liner'. In a system which separates strategy from operations the feedback loops, if they exist at all, are longer, more tenuous, more complex and infinitely less effective. If enterprises are constrained by external strategy to maintain course, to the extent that they are unable to make the constant stream of course corrections necessary, the enterprise is certain to go off course and the strategy will fail.

Other difficulties arise when the targets chosen are not, or cease to be, the main focus of public concern. Real concerns may, in practice, be difficult to identify and the targets chosen may be an inadequate representation. An aggregate national target may not focus attention on the concerns of specific communities and the individuals within it.

Even where targets are met the public may be unconvinced, tending to believe that statistics have been selected or manipulated to produce the desired result.

The lead time between a target being identified, plans drawn up and implemented, and the outcomes quantified, may be considerable. By such time, public priorities may have shifted and the results appear irrelevant. Meanwhile the continuing focus on the original target may have done much to contribute to an image of unresponsiveness on the part of the institution concerned.

The Public Accounts Committee has characterised the current accountability regime as 'a distraction focusing management attention up the hierarchy to meet the needs of policy makers rather than focusing down on the more immediate concerns of the consumers of their services.' The negative impact of such an approach is magnified in an environment which is subject to rapid change.

In learning and skills, as the pace of globalisation increases and industries can relocate, restructure, appear or disappear overnight, agility and the ability to react to unpredictable changes in the local demand for skills becomes increasingly important.

Strategic bodies can set a vision and they can try to determine the strategies and actions needed to move towards it. The actions taken will have a whole range of unpredictable consequences and the system will undoubtedly evolve in directions which were neither desired nor foreseen. Where strategy and operations are separated and communications between them are ineffective, the lack of feedback will ensure that the system is unable to react, it will inevitably become unresponsive and perhaps unstable.

In contrast to this, the central challenge for public services is to improve public perception through responding rapidly to the perceived needs and requirements of customers and communities. This, in turn, should drive decision-making, including decisions concerning the allocation of the resources available.

In order to achieve this public policy should adopt the following:

Broaden the range of informed decision-makers

The shortcomings of any individual decision-maker can be mitigated by increasing the number of agents involved in effective decision-making. This will allow a greater spread of evidence and perspectives to be reflected and taken forward. It will also reduce the impact of any single poor decision. The increase in processing power which results will itself be of value. James Surowiecki in, *The Wisdom of Crowds*,[2] argues that 'the many' will reach better decisions than 'the few' provided the following conditions are in place:

- they are reasonably informed (they do not have to be experts);
- they are independent;
- they are decentralised; and
- the means exist to reach a decision.

Shorten the feedback loop between customers and providers

This will improve the quality and speed of communication between both parties and crucially allow the corrective action to be taken at operational level when overarching strategies fail to achieve the desired result.

In the current model the feedback loop is heavily extended, with customer and stakeholder views channelled through layers of intermediary bodies through to the strategic centre before passing back, again through intermediaries, to the service providers themselves. The planning cycles are measured in years, whereas, as Alan Johnson observed at the November 2006 AoC conference, 'These days change happens in weeks, not years'.

All of this points towards the need to re-examine the case for devolving more decision-making down to levels closer to the customer. The comparison of decision-making today with the models developed during the 1990s tells its own story. In the 1990s funding in learning and skills and other public services 'followed the customer' and the planning and intervention roles of central funding agencies were kept to an absolute minimum.

Probably the worst thing that could happen to 1990s chief executives was that their customers would desert them, leading to a loss of confidence and, with all probability, to ensuing financial difficulties. In 2007 concerns will be dominated by inspectors and the new powers of intervention taken by the LSC, Strategic Health Authorities and others.

Strategic agencies may have developed mechanisms (usually samples or surveys) to ascertain what customers in aggregate think, but the food chain is longer and the environment infinitely more complex. In practice, the influence of individual customers on delivery, as distinct from those who claim to represent them, is, by any practical measure, negligible.

The views of those closest to the customer are also discounted as 'providers' rather than 'strategic partners'. They are characterised as acting in their own, rather than in the customer, interest. Those around the decision-making table seldom apply this criticism to themselves. If they did, the criticism would be no more or less valid.

The problems of the present, however, will not be solved purely through a return to the past. The 'customers' of incorporated colleges, apart from taking their business elsewhere (or nowhere), had precious little influence over the day-to-day decision-making in the institution. The needs of other stakeholders in the area who did not choose to become customers, perhaps because the institution had not developed an interest in their needs, hardly figured at all.

It appears, however, that the tide has begun to turn. Devolution is decidedly back in fashion. Local authorities, for one, sense an opportunity to make up lost ground. The Chairman of the Local Government Association (LGA), Sir Sandy Bruce-Lockhart, said at the LGA's 2005 annual conference: 'The time has come for audacious and deep-seated reform. All of our objectives are to improve public services, widening both access and choice, and offering opportunity for all...There is, however, a further challenge. We see an erosion of democracy, a crisis of trust, a cynicism with politicians and with the ability of seemingly unreachable governance to deliver solutions. We must give people back power and influence over their lives, their local services, and the future of the places where they live.'

The phrase 'double devolution' has been coined to describe a process by which power is first passed down, and then passed on, through successive layers of the democratic structure. There are, of course, potential pitfalls in this approach. In a multi-layered world each level will generate its own bureaucracy, infrastructure costs and inertia. When the inevitable conflict occurs, who decides? Will more layers and more structure invoke a law of diminishing returns? Will the public have any more confidence and trust in a local account-ability structure than a national one? The relative turnouts on national and local elections do not provoke optimism in this regard.

Perhaps an alternative mind-set is in order. Rather than starting at the top and devolving down, why not start at the bottom? To avoid the problems which arose in the 1990s in focusing exclusively on the direct consumers of a service, we should seek to develop a methodology which allows us to broaden our concerns to other stakeholders and interests who have a legitimate interest in the performance of any given public enterprise. The challenge would be to align as closely as possible the needs and expectations of local stakeholders with their perceptions of the quality of delivery of the service, while still allowing scope for policy-makers to sustain legitimate influence in areas where there are concerns at national level.

The focus is therefore on the value of the service as perceived by the public or, more precisely, 'the perceived value of a service as determined by the *considered* view of the *informed* citizen'. The words 'considered' and 'informed' are deliberate. They imply a duty on the service-provider to inform its customers and stakeholders on its performance and to debate its policy intentions with them. They also suggest that stakeholder rights are balanced by a responsibility to engage with the issues in a manner well beyond that envisaged by traditional 'knee-jerk' survey methodology.

The concept of public value is not new. It is already being field-tested in Northern Ireland, where the Department for Employment and Learning has announced its intention to implement the recommendations of a recent study by Chris Hughes into quality improvement methodology in further education and training in the Province.[3] Entitled *Purpose, Performance and Public Value*, it takes the concept of public value as its central theme and explores practical means by which the quality improvement model can be taken forward. Key recommendations include a shift in focus from narrowly-defined outputs to a broader view of outcomes, including the impact an institution has in achieving its clearly-defined purpose in the community it serves.

The Northern Ireland model goes some way into exploring how impact is to be measured in practice, with proposals for in-depth customer and stake-holder surveys, Benchmarking Clubs and the development of the NI College Information System. National developments on increasing the role of the learning voice may also prove helpful. There is a revised role for inspection with an emphasis on uncovering why things work. This information can then be shared with the sector and contribute to the improvement of standards overall. The whole emphasis is on assessing performance against purpose with attention focusing less on eliminating failure through mere compliance, and more on what it takes to encourage colleges to be at the top of their game. The improvement agency, in this case LSDA Northern Ireland, works within the system to take the work forward.

One can envisage building on this approach to the extent that colleges see their primary concern as responding to the wishes of their students, customers and local stakeholders, as more important than the outcomes of inspection and the achievement of national targets. Government at national or regional level would continue to express its policy goals and monitor the aggregate performance of the system. In summary it would adopt management best practice and 'trust but verify'. In reality public sector institutions are likely to be heavily influenced by the national and regional agenda but in the event of significant market failure funding agencies could retain the reserve power to commission new provision should it prove necessary.

If the primary goal of a provider, however, is to strive to identify and meet the real needs of the customers, communities and other stakeholders they serve, as opposed to concentrating on targets set remotely or other professional concerns, their reputation can only improve. One can envisage a 'balanced stakeholder scorecard' into which the mix of stakeholders and relative weighting given to each of them can be clearly articulated and the results reported.

The underlying drift of public sector reform runs parallel to moves to increase the power and engagement of citizens. If public institutions are to gain the trust and confidence of their customers and the communities and stakeholders that they seek to serve, they should be encouraged to shift their focus onto identifying and meeting their concerns and meeting their needs. They should not be overly distracted from this task by the demands and dictats of others. Institutions should clearly and transparently define their purpose, in terms of the groups, communities and stakeholders they seek to serve. They should develop a realistic view of the relative influence and priorities to be assigned to each of them. They should then seek to develop strong interactive relationships and the methodologies for sustaining them so that they are suitably informed, engaged and empowered in strategic decisions on priorities and resources. In this way quality, reputation, community involvement will go hand-in-hand.

In such a system the role of the various agencies involved would be clearly defined as follows:

Government Departments	• To determine and communicate broad policy priorities • To research and report on aggregate performance and impact at national level
Funding Agency	• To fund sufficient provision for which there is demand at local level • To determine the level of public subsidy which is appropriate/affordable • To research the market and commission additional provision where gaps are identified or where there is evidence that markets, communities and stakeholders are dissatisfied with the quality of provision on offer
Providers	• To identify clearly those markets, communities and stakeholders they commit to serve • To engage them in dialogue to ascertain their needs • To demonstrate to their satisfaction that they are adequately engaged in strategic and operational decision-making within the institution • To deliver to their satisfaction

For me, the ultimate test is the answer to a hypothetical question put to providers, 'What agencies are most critical to the future survival and success of your business?' Currently an honest answer to that question would probably focus on the outcomes of inspection or intervention by central government and its agencies. If they were instead able to point to the opinions and actions of their students, communities and stakeholders then the value the public place on their services could only improve.

Notes

1 Paul Ormerod, Why Most Things Fail, Evolution, Extinction and Economics, (2005).
2 James Surowiecki, The Wisdom of Crowds, (2004).
3 Chris Hughes, Purpose, Performance and Public Value, LSDA Northern Ireland (2005).

CHAPTER 6

Public value: international insights
TOM SCHULLER

The first point to establish is quite what we mean by 'public value'. I see three possible interpretations:

1. *Publicly shared beliefs or norms of a general kind,* for example in the importance of a tolerant society but one with clearly defined national values. The question then is what education's role should be in supporting these.
2. *Desirable – i.e. valued – features or goals of the education system,* for example in enabling a nation to compete in a global economy whilst at the same time sustaining solidarity between different social groups, generations, etc. Arguably, even the public articulation of these goals is itself a significant contribution.
3. *Value judgements about the best way of achieving 2.*

I don't have a view which of these should be given priority in the current exercise, but they do require rather different approaches. They could all do with systematic and sustained exploration.

What follows are more notes towards exploring some of these issues, referring partly to the international picture, at quite a generalised level, but including some rather idiosyncratic pointers to future issues.

First, some 'valuing' of what is happening in England or the UK (most of our OECD data refers to the UK, but I am certainly aware of how values differ within the nation). By valuing, I mean identifying areas where at least at one level, performance appears to be relatively good. I say this not out of a Panglossian desire to bolster morale, but because it is worth pointing to what looks a priori like good performance relative to other countries, in order to assess what needs to be done to maintain this – even if on closer inspection the performance may turn out not to be as strong as the figures suggest.

Figure 6.1 shows 'educational expectancy', with the UK very near the top of the figure. This is partly due to starting formal education relatively early (which gains us two years over most Scandinavian countries, for example), but it is some indication. Getting people into school early and keeping many of them there longer may not actually result in substantive achievement, but it suggests

---

Education expectancy (2003)

All levels of education from primary education to adult life,
excluding education for children under the age of five

Number of years

22 ▲	Australia (21.1)
21	Sweden (20.1), United Kingdom (20.4)
20	Iceland (19.2), Belgium and Finland (19.7)
19	Norway (18.2), Denmark (18.3), New Zealand (18.6)
18	Germany, Hungary and Poland (17.2), Netherlands (17.3) Spain (17.0)
17	Ireland, Switzerland (16.7), France, Italy, United States (16.8), Portugal
16	(16.9) Austria (16.1), Korea (16.4), Greece (16.5), Czech Republic (16.6) Slovak Republic (15.3)
15	Luxembourg (14.8)
14	Mexico (13.2)
13	
12	Turkey (12.0)

Figure 6.1. (Source OECD)

that there is a commitment to education. It is worth noting that countries with high proportions of non-native speakers see early schooling as a crucial route to social integration.

Of course, long educational expectancy may largely signal an extended period of initial education, rather than effective lifelong learning. But Figure 6.2 is quite powerful evidence on the higher education opportunities given to 30- to 39-year-olds, with the UK actually in pole position. A pessimistic interpretation of this might refer to the catch-up needed on countries which have higher enrolment rates amongst the 20- to 29-year-olds, but here the lifelong learning argument goes the other way, i.e. the UK does appear to offer more opportunities.

Figure 6.3 deals with participation in continuing education by labour force members. The UK comes out reasonably well on this – and on estimates of amounts spent on continuing education as a proportion of wage bills. This may be a surprise. Of course, both quantity and quality remain in question. We can ask, in relation to participation, how long the spells of education are – there is some indication that the UK goes for short spells – and whether the opportunities that these data denote are tied to narrow skills, but the figures in themselves are not depressing.

Figure 6.4 gives private expenditure on tertiary education. Why is this relevant? Partly in the sense that it's a proxy for people's willingness to spend on

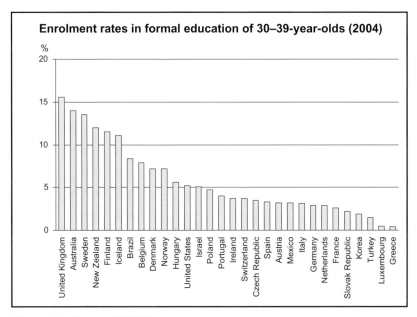

Figure 6.2. (Source OECD)

education, beyond what is invested in their name through state expenditure. Korean levels are extraordinary, and reflect a valuing of education which is, arguably, unhealthily intense (i.e. Korean children spent a huge number of hours on additional schooling, on a daily basis). Within this variety there is no ideal mixture of public and private, but a debate on values must bring into the frame the issue of how we prefer to see learning financed; and especially for citizens to debate how far it should be financed through the state or through other means. A strong debate on this would be healthy, even though it is far from sure that it would be encouraging for those of us who believe that all should be in favour of public and private spending on adult education. NIACE has done valuable work on this already.

Tertiary data also indicate the changes which are occurring in the levels of graduate output, with China, Russia and Brazil all with large populations and increasing their numbers of graduates by around 10 per cent annually. Personally I am sceptical about an over-emphasis on the supply side, but in a globalised economy it reminds us that we need to pay attention to what is happening elsewhere, even if these figures may disguise major issues of quality.

So much for figures, which suggest that there is much to be done but there is no need to wring hands in total despair. Now for some reflections under loosely related headings, which I hope point to areas where innovative work might follow from thinking about values.

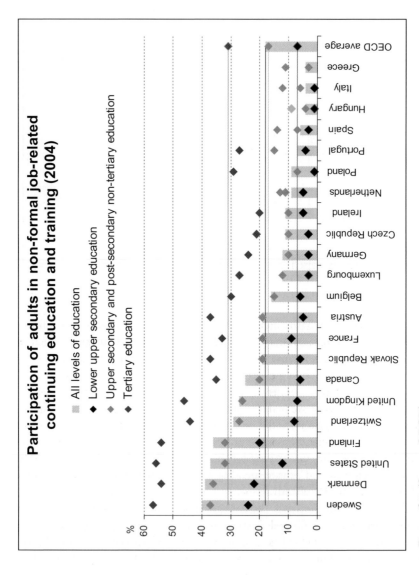

Figure 6.3. (Source OECD)

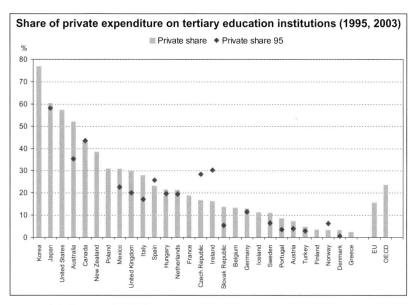

Figure 6.4. (Source OECD)

Building social capital

Bridging social capital refers to links made to people unlike ourselves, on whatever dimension is considered relevant. The bridge may be across ethnic, social or generational divides. To take just the last: there are enormous advantages to be gained in maintaining and strengthening a sense of solidarity across generations, and education of many different kinds can play a big part in this. Parents' attitudes to education are a major influence on their children's achievements. Generally this is a positive influence, at least at the individual level. But it also accentuates inequalities, as those with educated parents tend to get more encouragement – another reason why any strategy which focuses only on the young is fundamentally flawed. Grandparents and other elders can both help in the same direction but also sustain their own sense of worth and autonomy through involvement, as the Swedish Grandads scheme illustrates. More generally, the more a society as a whole feels a stake in education, the more likely we are to avoid a dystopian unwillingness to contribute through taxation to the education of others. Intensifying competition for public expenditure, notably on health as a function of ageing populations, make this a very significant public value issue.

Collective consumerism

Michael Young's extraordinary insights into the political need to go with the grain of consumerism remain with us. Consumerism can take many different forms, and these need not all be to do with winning the best deal for ourselves as individual purchasers of goods or services. Many of us wish to have our voices heard as consumers of public services in order that the service may improve – for ourselves, certainly but also for our fellow citizens. If we suffer poor service from our local hospital, for example, extracting financial compensation may be fair enough, but pooling our feedback to ensure better future treatment is more attractive and sustainable. Learning how to do this constructively and effectively is an interesting challenge, and a legitimate one for education. There is much scope here for linking up with consumer bodies such as the National Consumers Council, to promote the skills and attitudes needed to support a creative consumerism which supports collective services.

Positive-sum competition

Can we avoid a polarisation between those who favour competition and those who oppose it? In appropriate structures and contexts, competition is healthy and results in improved services and higher levels of job satisfaction for most of those involved. This is important for a number of reasons, including bridging the producer-consumer divide. Valuing that kind of positive-sum game, whilst being alert to the downsides of dysfunctional forms of competition, is going to make a big difference to the quality of education. Like it or not (and I do), the programme *Strictly Come Dancing* shows that fierce and determined competition can happen with healthy mutual support. (SCD's other educational virtue is to show how initially incompetent people can put themselves on the line to learn.)

Innovation and continuity

The UK, as elsewhere, has educational traditions of which it can be proud – adult education being one of them. Maintaining the tradition of so-called seriously useless knowledge – of public provision and of learning unrelated to qualifications – is an enormous value issue. Once such a tradition is lost it is hard to recapture. At the same time, innovation is needed which may challenge some of our cherished assumptions about how best to deliver learning opportunities, and about how to ensure that these opportunities are distributed reasonably and equitably. Some countries – the UK amongst them – are historically better at invention than innovation; that is to say, they seem to have poor cultures and mechanisms for implementing change, especially systemic change. We do not know enough about how innovation works, and how we can turn good ideas into good practice. Paying attention to this, and building a knowledge base to encourage innovation in education, is an issue of values as well as practice.

CHAPTER 7

Doing the wrong thing righter?

RICHARD HOOPER

Introduction

This chapter was originally commissioned on the understanding that the working title should be 'Local government: the highways, byways and picnic areas of adult learning'. This only goes to prove the old rule that you should never provide the title before you have completed the work, although I have managed to contrive a reference to this original theme toward the end.

However, the more I thought about the topic the more I became exercised about the past and present role of local government in adult learning. Increasingly it seemed to me that something of the public value of adult learning has been lost with the erosion of influence of local government since the late 1980s. At the same time the emergence from *purdah* of the White Paper on local government and the steady revelation of thinking in progress from the Lyons review rekindled hopes that there might be a chance to reposition local government within a sector with which it has long and honourable association.

What follows, therefore, is no more than a reflection on the extent to which the public value of adult learning has been narrowed and constrained by a Skills Strategy which has lost sight of the deeper roots that adult learning should have in our local communities and in our lives as citizens rather than consumers and workers.

In making these reflections I have regard to the context provided by the other papers produced for this series of seminars and so have eschewed statistics and focussed on structures instead. I have also taken as axiomatic that good adult learning is a public good and as such should be made as freely or as cheaply available as possible. If a society or a Treasury needs to reduce subsidies to adult learning then perhaps we should first critically examine other activities in the public sector which soak up resources such as military interventions abroad or wasteful and uncoordinated transport systems.

Goodbye to all that

Well over one hundred years ago a member of the Poor Law Commission of 1833 said:

> 'The only rational foundation of government is expediency – the general benefit of the community. It is the duty of government to do whatever is conducive to the welfare of the governed.'[1]

The New Poor Law of 1834 was, to quote Dominic Hobson,

> '. . .the first instance in British history of legislation designed to achieve uniform results throughout the country by using centrally devised rules and centralised funding to eliminate local discretion.'[2]

From that moment on the involvement of central government grew through the creation and funding of unelected local quangos – health boards, highways boards, school boards and so forth. The only new thing about 'quangos' is the name.

By the time democratically-elected local government was established at the end of the nineteenth century they were already agents of government. They were given significant powers but if they failed then their powers became statutory duties. As perceived backsliding and inactivity became evident – in areas of health, sanitation, housing and schooling – so the statutory duties on local authorities grew and centralised control increased. Under Margaret Thatcher and successive governments dissatisfaction with the perceived messiness of local government has tended to lead to the reduction of statutory responsibilities and the parcelling-out of functions to quangos and/or private sector providers.

There is an inevitable circularity to all of this. In time central government has grown even more uneasy with the diversity and untidiness of local government, and particularly with its perceived propensity to contribute to inflation by spending more than it should. Just as nature abhors a vacuum so ministers abhor untidy local government and its never-ending reform remains their obsession. Today unelected quangos spend more public money than elected local authorities.

For all of these reasons and more, the responsibility of local government for further and higher education (the then polytechnics) was removed in 1993 under the Further and Higher Education Act 1992 and passed to the Further Education Funding Council. Regional training and economic development passed to Training and Enterprise Councils and Local Enterprise Companies. The one small exception was a requirement for local authorities to continue to provide adult learning of a non-vocational nature, the famous (or infamous) 'Non-Schedule 2'. This area of adult learning – significant for being defined in terms of what it is not rather than what it is – was all that remained. Even that concession was achieved only by the intervention of groups for which so called 'leisure' adult education was important, of which the National Federation of Women's Institutes was a major player.

The justification for these changes was thin. The then Secretary of State for Education and Science, Kenneth Clarke, announced to the House of Commons that although the Education Reform Act 1988 had given colleges greater management autonomy, they were:

> '. . .still subject to bureaucratic controls from local authorities. They lack the full freedom which we gave the polytechnics and higher education colleges in 1989b to respond to the demands of students and of the labour market.'

A predecessor of mine in Lancashire, Chris Brooks, offered this view of the assumption behind the removal of the further education colleges from local authority control:

> 'The message which the White Paper clearly conveyed was the Government's belief that a further education sector of this kind would be achieved more rapidly and sustained more successfully without the continued involvement of the local education authorities. The values characterised by local government – equity in resource allocation, co-ordination and planning across wide areas, equality of opportunity, and control of inter-institutional competition – would not deliver this kind of further education sector. It was not freedom from local authority bureaucracy or the analogy with polytechnics which motivated Government policy, but a desire to promote a sector in which market-related disciplines, incentives, accountabilities and pressures would create greater effectiveness, efficiency and economy.'[3]

Audit trails and the dash for growth

This prescient observation should be considered at some length in the light of the developments which have attended further and adult learning in the 16 years since the incorporation of the sector. For a brief period the Further Education Funding Council enabled opportunities for learners, including adults with learning difficulties, to become less a postcode lottery as its funding methodology and convergence was rolled out. As Leisha Fullick has observed:

> 'The FEFC certainly made mistakes. Its obsession with audit trails created a new, but equally burdensome, bureaucratic quagmire to some of those it had cleared away. Its rush for growth through franchising led some colleges into disaster from which a few never recovered. But above all it acted.'[4]

The interesting point is that FEFC was perceived, despite its many virtues, as 'burdensome and bureaucratic'. It was then dissolved and no doubt as part of a 'new broom' approach by a new administration wishing to sweep away some of the legacy of the old.

Red tape in the sunset

Now in 2007 we are watching the effective and radical reshaping of its successor, the Learning and Skills Council. The perplexity for many in the local authority sector is that over a decade after their fingers were prised from the levers of control of adult learning the then Secretary State for Education and Skills, another Clarke, required an independent Bureaucracy Task Force under Sir George Sweeney to say there must be 39 ways to leave the 'red tape mountain' – as the song-writer Paul Simon might have put it and Sir George in fact did.

Doing the wrong things righter

At this point the question 'why should this be the case?' needs to be asked and answered. An audit trail – dread phrase – of the evolution of adult learning funding since 1 April 1993 would provide an answer. However, I shall provide some bureaucracy-busting of my own and offer a model borrowed *via* Simon Caulkin of *The Observer* from the systems theorist Russ Ackoff, which may help to provide an analytical tool to help understand what has happened.

Adult learning, like much of the public sector, now exists in a ferment and culture of managerialism. This is like bureaucracy except that it is promoted not by local authorities but by a management industry of consultants, gurus, applied private sector case studies and of course software solutions. Indeed Caulkin observes wryly that 'If a problem can be expressed in words, someone will write a software "solution" to manage it'.[5]

The key point, however, is made by Ackoff in that we find ourselves doing 'the wrong thing righter'. This, I would suggest, is where the macro-management of adult learning is at the present time. It is worth quoting him in full in the context of what has been said before:

> 'The righter we do the wrong thing, the wronger we become. When we make a mistake doing the wrong thing and correct it, we become wronger. When we make a mistake doing the right thing and correct it, we become righter. Therefore it is better to do the right thing wrong than the wrong thing right.'[6]

It is also worth applying Ackoff's conclusion about the centralisation of the economy to the specifics of adult learning: 'We are committed to a market economy at the national [macro] level and to a non-market, centrally planned, hierarchically managed [micro] economy within most corporations.' For corporations read 'adult learning providers' – whether colleges of further education, private training providers, or local authority adult education services.

Caulkin concludes that in a culture where each effort to control the uncontrollable simply destabilises the system further, the end of management becomes control rather than the creation of resources.

Skills Strategy: the Laws of Unintended Consequences

I firmly believe that in the Skills Strategy, in itself a sound but limited aspiration and project, we already can see evidence that we are trying to do 'the wrong thing righter' as the marginalisation of liberal and community adult learning proceeds, as thousands of adult learning places are displaced by arbitrary skills priorities, and the potential emergence of deadwood funding within brokered training programmes emerges. Skills Councils evolve their own well-intended bureaucracies and although the employer voice will undoubtedly win through, the potential for sclerosis in the system is ever present. The deeper malaise of doing the wrong thing righter has manifested itself through structural reform after structural reform in the sector since 1993 (and before) through the Law of Unintended Consequences and its concomitant the Law of Too Many Moving Parts.

Local government: still here – but only just

Today central government provides 80 per cent of what local government spends, an expenditure which itself is tightly and minutely regulated and monitored through legislative coercion. Meanwhile the role of local government has continued in its evolution as an agent of government, as an enabling authority and more recently as 'Local Government PLC' in respect of its structure and process, the emphasis on cabinet government – for cabinet read 'board of directors' and for chief executive read, well, 'chief executive'.

Incidentally, you may have begun to wonder at this point if you have strayed into the wrong seminar. What has the transformation of the role of local government in its generality got to do with the development of adult learning, and especially the value of adult learning in particular? Well, apart from the fact that unless we know our history we are doomed to repeat it, then quite a lot because we have been witnessing the almost complete elimination from adult learning of the power, influence and involvement of local government and that, as I intend to go on to illustrate, bodes ill for the sector.

Those were the days

In 1998 the young New Labour Government published a Green Paper – *The Learning Age* – which appeared to recognise and regenerate the holistic and civic base of adult learning. It has been quoted many times but it is worth reminding ourselves of some of the key assumptions and intentions that informed it. First that the Government's vision was more than just about employment:

> *'As well as securing our economic future, learning has a wider contribution. It helps makes ours a civilised society, develops the spiritual side of our lives and promotes active citizenship. Learning helps people to play a full part in their community. It strengthens the family, the neighbourhood and consequently the nation. It helps us fulfil our potential and opens doors to a love of music, art and literature. That is why we value learning for its own sake as well as for the equality of opportunity that it brings.'[7]*

It went on to identify the value of adult learning for different groups in society.

> *'For individuals, in their advance to better employability, learning offers excitement and the opportunity for discovery. It stimulates enquiring minds and nourishes our souls. It takes us in directions we never expected, sometimes changing our lives. Learning helps create and sustain our culture. It helps older people to stay healthy and active, strengthens families and the wider community, and encourages independence. There are many people for whom learning has opened up, for the first time in their lives, the chance to explore art, music, literature, film, and the theatre, or to become creative themselves.'*

For businesses, learning drove productivity and national competitive advantage. For communities, learning contributed to social cohesion and fostered a sense of belonging, responsibility and identity, and helped them to respond to economic and social change. For the nation, lifelong learning lay at the heart of the Government's welfare reform programme. The Government wished to bridge the 'learning divide' and break a 'vicious circle of under-achievement, self-deprecation, and petty crime.'

Ah yes, local government . . . mmm, ah, well . . .

The Green Paper also declared that local authorities would play a major role in helping to carry forward learning throughout life. Local authorities, it was pointed out, act as providers, coordinators and supporters of lifelong learning in many different ways. The Government also announced it would be consulting with the Local Government Association about how the contribution of local authorities can best be focused, including through Education Development Plans and strategic planning with other major partners. That role is perhaps better defined in the 14–19 phase at present than in the adult learning sector [and now to be reinforced by assuming a funding role for 16–19 provision from 2009].

Learning for Life

The final report of NIACE's Committee of Enquiry: Adult Learning in Further Education Colleges – a thoughtful enterprise albeit largely, but not entirely, local authority-free both in representation or reference – commented on the distance travelled since the publication of *The Learning Age* in 1998 and the current Skills Strategy and pointed out that the emphasis is much more utilitarian.

> '. . . much of the strategy shaping post-compulsory education and training – apart from in the field of higher education – is about skills acquisition.'[8]

This is true and the effect of priority-led funding, the continued diversion of resources to a declining 16–18 cohort in defiance of immediate demographic trends, and the dominance of economic performance as the significant goal of learning has led, or is leading, to the marginalisation of the wider value of adult learning as an essential ingredient of social cohesion, civic engagement and healthy – in all senses – communities.

Incidentally, here is an example of another law to brigade with the Law of Unintended Consequences and the Law of Too Many Moving Parts: the Law of Swiftly Passed-Over and Uncontested Assumptions.

The Law of Swiftly Passed-Over and Uncontested Assumptions

The Law of Swiftly Passed Over and Uncontested Assumptions states that if you say something often enough and in small enough paragraphs in official reports then in time you will be able to base substantial policies upon them without challenge.

Like the discredited 'trickle-down effect' of wealth distribution promoted by Friedmanite monetarists in the 1980s, the LSC's assumption is that 'the concentration on skills needn't mean a dilution of the social role of education in our society. Indeed the best route to social inclusion is through employability.'[9] Oh no, it isn't! Oh yes it is!

The point here is that there is sufficient truth in the proposition for it to have legs – but the legs cannot support the contention that employability is the 'best' route, nor the loosely-implied conclusion that it may be the 'only' route. There are many other routes to social inclusion and some of them start in non-vocational settings for people with mental ill-health; for some adults with learning difficulties; for older people reaching out to the community following long illness or bereavement; for people beginning to assemble the building blocks of confidence after a childhood and young adulthood of failure, drug addiction or imprisonment. Employability can provide confidence, independence and progression, and, if the earnings and outgoings balance, it can contribute to less social exclusion than a state of unemployment. But let us not stretch the elastic of credibility to the point where it becomes a sufficient substitute for other targeted interventions of which adult and community learning, the so-called personal and community development stream, is one.

I have rehearsed previously on another public platform a view that the prioritisation of adult learning for skills over all other purposes is based on another misleading assumption. This is that economic prosperity and international competitiveness are a direct and important consequence of the acquisition of skills levels as measured by the level and focus of vocational qualifications. The Leitch review will undoubtedly confirm Government, LSC and employer views that we need a higher platform of skills and that these are linked to long-term prosperity. There is much in this view that can be supported but it needs to be seen in the context of other, more significant determinants of economic prosperity: technological advance; fiscal management; movements of capital flows; national patterns of consumption *versus* investment; political developments. The looming economic significance of China and India has not flowed chiefly or significantly from a long-term investment in vocational training but from deeper, more fundamental changes in their politics and readiness to align their natural advantage in cheap labour to market development.

Yet the Skills Strategy is based on this largely unchallenged assumption, under the weight of which an entire swathe of valuable adult learning – and its infrastructure – is in danger of being rolled upon and flattened.

The need for a lifelong learning strategy

A key finding of the NIACE-commissioned report was that although we have a Skills Strategy and a Minister and Director General for Lifelong Learning, we have no strategy for lifelong learning. Among the many issues that it urged the Government to address were:

- the need for more strategic collaboration between colleges, businesses, community organisations, local authorities and LSCs;
- a need for further education to reclaim space for strategic intervention and for the LSC role to be less directive and more enabling;
- flexible curricula to transform local skills economies; and
- the need for a lifelong learning strategy to complement that for skills.

Déjà vu, anyone?

To take these macro-recommendations and splice them to the re-introduction of Full-Time Equivalent employees, the abandonment of claw-back and the introduction of plan-led funding enables us to step into a time-capsule and travel back to the 1988 Education Reform Act. The only significant change is that in 1988 all adult learning was equally valued and regarded as interlinked. Oh, and of course, it was local authorities, not the LSC, who were being asked to be more enabling and less directive.

My point is not, therefore, that the interests of adult learning in both its vocational and wider social purpose were better served under local government and that all that has transpired since 1993 has been detrimental. There have been significant benefits to adult learning not least in the national profile it has achieved; the drive for quality; increased support and emphasis on professionalism for teachers; capital investment and better technological resources.

However, I do believe that many of these benefits could have been achieved, and many of the mistakes and wasted energy and resources borne of frequent restructuring of quango-ism avoided, through a proper and rigorous exercise of statutory duties and powers through the framework of local government. In other words we could have avoided the last 14 years of making things wronger by trying to make them righter, and focused on trying not to do the right thing wronger.

It is clear that the Independent Committee of Enquiry is right: we need a national strategy for lifelong learning of which employer-focused skills acquisition is an important but complementary provision, and with a priority for other adult learning which is recognised by an appropriate funding allocation and for which discretion is devolved locally.

As I stumble toward a conclusion I do not propose to detail what a lifelong learning strategy should be but simply to adumbrate what the key principles should be. I also propose that the statutory role of enabling and coordinating a lifelong learning strategy, as distinct from funding or managing further education colleges, should be returned to local authorities.

Towards a lifelong learning strategy

A lifelong learning strategy has to subsume a skills strategy. To regard skills acquisition as separate from community or cultural learning misses the point. The point is, as NIACE has repeatedly stated, and as all adult learning providers know, that adults do not necessarily progress through learning in a linear fashion. To quote the Learning for Life report again:

'It is time for new thinking, new vocabulary. Lifelong learning is not a phased-out policy ambition; it is a reality and a necessity. In truth, it is a fact of contemporary life, but we fail to harness learning in all its forms, formal and informal, vocational and general, learning to know and learning to do – we need to stop regarding the different phases of teaching and learning as independent and isolated, as being in some way in competition. We need to think through the organisational consequences of what learning through life really means.'

I feel like many others that this is a message acknowledged in the rhetoric of government, given lip service by funding priorities, but not fully comprehended or valued by many people who occupy positions of influence in the planning and funding infrastructure. In a misplaced rush for economic prosperity through vocational training we are in danger of elbowing aside our potential as learning and civic communities. The two are not mutually exclusive – indeed they are highly complementary.

The value of adult learning

In Lancashire I had until recently overall responsibility for a group of services which include not only adult learning but also museums and heritage, libraries and information services; community arts development; records and archives; student transport and higher education services. At the last count we found ourselves working with over 3,000 local community stakeholders and partners including other local authorities, community, faith and voluntary organisations, companies, and many others. Our learning paths are interlinked. Adults can travel the motorways of our Lancashire Adult Learning Service, explore the pathways provided by the People's Network of our libraries, time-travel through our museums, trace their personal and community history through our records and archives service; pause in the picnic areas of our community arts, performance and drama services.

This group of services not only interacts seamlessly with themselves but also links across to our adult social care services – we are in the same Directorate – so that adult learning, whether through formal LSC-funded provision or through cultural services activities, can be linked to older people, people with mental ill-health and adults with learning difficulties. The goals of our services are not simply expressed in learning outcomes but in terms of social cohesion, of the wellbeing of our local communities.

The joy is that we can see the potential of providing seamless adult learning through wider social and community engagement and are enabled to do so. The frustration is in facing the relentless erosion and narrowing of focus of our LSC resources, and the lack of resources or freedom to 'bend' resources to provide truly joined-up adult and community learning.

The value of learning to adults is holistic. We cannot arbitrarily separate the benefits of adult learning into skills acquisition, confidence, health, individual and civic wellbeing, family and community cultures and many more. All of these are interlinked and different, within each individual's life-journey. It is similarly false to separate rigidly or prioritise the funding to encourage narrow outcomes. To do so fails to recognise how adults work and play in their daily lives, or take account of the different roles they play from hour to hour as work colleagues, parents, grandparents, consumers, voters, community activists, patients and many more.

The value of adult learning as an activity with a social purpose – as distinct from a merely vocational or economic one – requires re-emphasis, possibly rediscovery. The thrust of the recently-published White Paper *on Local Government: Strong and Prosperous Communities*[10] is about the greater engagement of citizens with local affairs and the assertion of local community interest. There is at the heart of the White Paper's intentions a desire to improve democracy and promote equality, to support and champion the individual and smaller community interests and enable them to assert their interests and views. This is wholly welcome but to achieve these ends the intention requires support for the capacity of individuals and small communities to engage. The development of this capacity through adult learning necessarily involves familiar and presently funded and prioritised provision: skills for life and other vocational support which enables people to read, write and understand reports, acquire confidence in meetings, analyse figures, plan campaigns, submit bids, draw up business plans for community centres and so forth.

The model, however, is close to that described by Ian Martin in a recent article in *Adults Learning* lamenting the loss of social purpose in adult learning in which he refers to contemporary educational work as: 'essentially concerned with helping people, especially marginalised individuals, to cope and survive rather than to understand and challenge the structures which oppress them. The learning process is adaptive rather than transformative. The consequence is a diminished and demoralised view of the autonomy and agency of both students and educators.'[11]

At present the public value of adult learning, and its funding, appears to have shrunk to a narrow view of learners as consumers of private and public services; as means to an economic and globally-competitive end. The emphasis is, if I can borrow from Ian Martin again, on transmitting to adult learners rather than engaging in dialogue with them; and on treating them as learners rather than as the 'social actors' they in fact are.

However, the view of adult learning needs to be far wider, as indeed it once was, and should also encompass its ability to enable people to understand critically their social and political context as a basis for action, challenge and political engagement.

The present arrangements place much emphasis on the price of providing adult learning – and no-one can argue that scarce resources do not require thoughtful management – but give the impression that a large area of adult learning is not valued. The description of someone who knows the price of everything and the value of nothing would be unfairly applied to those responsible for national policy. However, there is a danger that their policies may increasingly become seen as cynical.

Policies which serve to support adult learning clearly need to have regard to the economic benefits to which skills attainment leads. However, a skills strategy must be integrated within a broader learning for life vision which ranges over every aspect of learning in health, in social care, in community development, in culture. The one cannot be subordinated to the other. This requires a major commitment by central government to join its departments together so as to ensure that lifelong learning is provided and supported in a way that reflects and recognises the complexity and diversity of how we live our lives.

To achieve this at local level what better than to place a statutory duty to promote and secure adequacy in adult learning on the single organisation available which has the democratic locus and capacity to do so: local government. This would be to follow a direction of travel likely to be reinforced by the new White Paper on local government.

Local government – the opportunity

The publication of the long-awaited White Paper and the complementary Lyons report on local government offers an opportunity to address the task of creating a true learning for life strategy that helps to knit together these strands of economic, civic and community wellbeing.

The White Paper clearly indicates an intention for powers for the economic and civic wellbeing of communities to be devolved further from central to local government, and from local government to communities. The emphasis will be on a Sustainable Community Strategy and Local Development Frameworks.

There is an intention to give local authorities through Local Strategic Partnerships:

- a statutory duty to prepare a Local Area Agreement and a legal duty on specified public organisations – including the LSC – to cooperate with this;
- a greater leadership role in Local Strategic Partnerships and their thematic sub-partnerships; and
- extended powers to scrutinise other local agencies and ensure that their strategies are integrated in ways that promote community engagement.

Prime Minister Gordon Brown has now announced that local authorities will now, once again, be asked to fund 16–19 provision in schools and further education colleges (except for 16–19 apprenticeships) under the aegis of the new Department for Children, Schools and Families. How long will it be until local authorities are asked to assume a strategic planning role as well is anybody's guess. However, the continued separation of planning and funding between the LSC and local authorities is not tenable and it is clear that the LSC's days are numbered in this area of provision at least.

This will leave the new Department of Innovation, Universities and Skills [DIUS] responsible for science, research and innovation focused on achieving a world-class skills base (Leitch Review of Skills). This will include development, funding and performance management of higher education (teaching and research) and further education working closely with the Department for Children, Schools and Families. DIUS will 'sponsor' the Learning and Skills Council.

The big challenge here will be the reconciliation of the identified learning needs of empowered communities with the narrow priorities of the national Skills Strategy. In his argument for localism Sir Michael Lyons has already said that: '. . .it is simplistic to define "fairness" in public services as meaning the existence of a uniform national set of public services and uniform national set of priorities for the improvement of those services, whatever the opinions or priorities of local people.'[12]

He goes on to suggest that one of the key areas of debate required is the role of local councils with regard to economic development and skills investment.

There is major potential here for local authorities to reassert a senior strategic partnership role in ensuring that lifelong learning and skills strategies are planned at local level and linked with other agendas including community wellbeing, health, economic development, cultural services, social services, community and voluntary sectors, Every Child Matters and all of the many other services and functions for which local government has statutory interests and responsibilities.

However, if this is to be achieved there will have to be either a significant review and relaxation of the current adult learning funding regime or a crude increase in the amount of money available to 'social purpose' community-driven education.

Above all, the increased and direct involvement of local government in shaping and influencing adult learning might restore the democratic link which has been markedly missing from the past 14 years of 'making the wrong thing righter.' It is always perplexing to hear the view that because voter turnout can be less than 50 per cent in local elections then important services such as adult and further education are better entrusted to wholly unelected quangos. We are constantly looking to find new and innovative ways to give expression to the voice of the learner. Perhaps properly empowered local elected representatives of the learners in their communities might not be a bad idea to revisit.

Notes

1 Nassau Senior, Victorian economist. Quoted in Hobson, D. (1999) *The National Wealth*. Harper Collins.
2 Hobson, Dominic (1999) *The National Wealth*. Harper Collins.
3 Brooks, Chris (1993) *Education and the Law*. (Edited by Robert Morris), Longman.
4 Fullick, Leisha (2004) *Adult Learners in a Brave New World*. NIACE.
5 Caulkin, Simon 'The More We Manage, The Worse We Make Things', *The Observer*, 1 October 2006.
6 Russ Ackoff.
7 HMSO (1998) *The Learning Age: A Renaissance for a New Britain*. HMSO.
8 *Adult Learning in Further Education Colleges*, NIACE, (Independent Committee of Enquiry 2005).
9 *Success for All Bulletin* Issue 20, January/February 2006.
10 White Paper: *Local Government: Strong and Prosperous Communities* HMSO, 2006.
11 Martin, Ian (2006) 'Where have all the flowers gone?', *Adults Learning*, October 2006.
12 Sir Michael Lyons, *National Prosperity, Local Choice and Civic Engagement*. Executive summary/Interim Report.

CHAPTER 8

Public value and leadership – exploring the implications
CAROLINE MAGER

Introduction

This chapter has been prepared in order to stimulate discussion about the role of leadership in the evolving FE system. The growing body of thinking on public value explores the role of the public service leader in creating outcomes that are considered desirable by the public. The theory proposes that the objective of public sector leaders should be to use their resource to maximise their contribution to the public realm and to the achievement of outcomes valued by the public. To achieve this objective they need to engage with their citizens and direct customers to agree what constitutes public value in that particular public service and in that specific context.

Significantly, the theory challenges us to think about how we gain legitimacy for our actions as public service leaders, and suggests that this is derived from our relationship with our citizens, customers and stakeholders as well as from the delivery of government priorities. This suggests a shift in orientation towards the communities we serve – not just our customers and funding government departments – and towards our relationships with stakeholders such as other public services where we can make a contribution.

CEL believes that public value theory has the potential to provide a conceptual framework through which to analyse and develop the role of leaders in the FE system, particularly in the context of more autonomy for colleges and providers and the move towards greater self-regulation in the FE system. It promotes proactive leadership based on ambitious vision and is consistent with more autonomous and self-regulating colleges and providers. This chapter explores this potential and proposes how its practical application might be taken forward in the FE system.

Background

Professor Mark Moore from Harvard[1] originated the concept of public value and became involved in the UK through Professor John Benington, Professor of Public Policy and Management at Warwick Business School, and Will Hutton, Chief Executive at The Work Foundation. Moore has worked with opinion-formers in the UK, including senior members of Government, and Benington and Hutton have raised the profile and developed the concept for the UK context. As a result, there is increasing debate and application of thinking about public value among the leadership of public services.

There has been some analysis of the relevance of the concepts specifically to the FE system. In 2005, Mager and Grigg published a stimulus paper, *Public Value and Learning and Skills*,[2] that described the main tenets of thinking on public value. The publication generated particular interest in how public value might be used to describe the value created through public services in a more complete and compelling manner. We have grown accustomed to public services being judged in terms of narrow targets that do not do justice to their purpose or their contribution to economic, social and environmental well-being. Public value theory highlights the importance of taking a more holistic view of the purposes of public services.

While this remains an important and controversial area, current thinking on public value in the UK suggests that the *process* of public value creation is fundamental. Through the deliberative process of negotiating what constitutes public value in a specific context, public value is defined and created. This dimension of public value is particularly germane to leadership. For example, it:

- places agency with leaders and managers in their context;
- animates the notion of engagement with customers and communities;
- highlights the importance of gaining legitimacy and authorisation for action;
- provides a conceptual basis for leadership in a self-regulating environment; and
- offers a public service compass within a market-driven system.

Public value – the theory to date

Moore's publication offers the following description of what public value might provide:

> 'A framework that helps us connect what we believe is valuable. . .and requires public resources, with improved ways of understanding what our "publics" value and how we connect to them.'[3]

In essence Moore presents public value thinking as a means of focusing public services on delivering ends that are endorsed and supported by service users and their communities. The role of the public service leader is to maximise the amount of public value created, within their given remit. Moore argues that in shaping proposals for the development of a public service, the leader needs to consider:

- whether the proposed outcome is publicly valuable;
- whether it will be politically and legally supported; and
- whether it is administratively and operationally feasible.

Moore's strategic triangle represents this diagrammatically, setting out the dimensions that the public service leader or manager needs to consider in developing a course of action:

- the **authorising or political environment** – for example, ensuring that customers, stakeholders, sponsors and funders support the proposed action;
- the **operational capacity** – ensuring that the organisation has the operational capacity, skills and competences to carry out the proposed action; and
- **public value, strategic goals** – ensuring that the action is in line with the values, mission and purpose of the organisation.

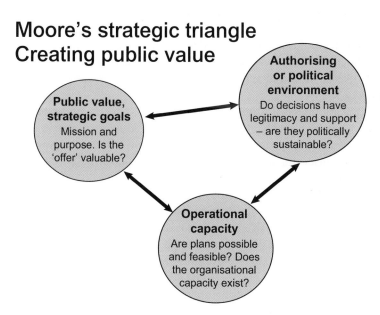

Moore's strategic triangle
Creating public value

Authorising or political environment
Do decisions have legitimacy and support – are they politically sustainable?

Public value, strategic goals
Mission and purpose. Is the 'offer' valuable?

Operational capacity
Are plans possible and feasible? Does the organisational capacity exist?

The proposition in the strategic triangle is that purpose, capacity and legitimacy (which would include customer demand) must be aligned in order to provide the public manager or leader with the necessary authority to create public value through a particular course of action. This would equally be true of the private sector, although the concern would be with creating shareholder value rather than public value. The *scope* of the authorising environment and the *process* of seeking authorisation are key to Moore's proposition.

Moore makes an important distinction between 'clients' – direct customers – and citizens. He argues that in order to introduce a radical or challenging change in public services (for example, changing the use of a public building, or introducing new charging policies) robust support is needed not just by those who will benefit directly but from the wider community within which the services are delivered. So, for example, taxpayers may support the provision of sheltered housing, a children's library, a youth activity or playground facility because they recognise the value to their community or wider society, even if they do not personally use the services concerned. Implicitly these taxpayers are accepting that these services make a positive contribution to the society they live in which they are willing to pay for.

Moore's work suggests that this public acceptance needs to be sought explicitly and deliberately to establish robust authority for action. If this authorisation is not achieved, then the enterprise is vulnerable to public criticism and susceptible to being abandoned and losing the necessary political support. In order to achieve this authorisation, there needs to be a process of engagement and deliberation which encourages individuals to take an informed and wider perspective of the social and public outcomes of particular transactions and services.

This is not intended to suggest that customer views are unimportant. Customers' feedback is vitally important in understanding users' desires and priorities for service improvement but their satisfaction will not necessarily deliver public legitimacy for a specific service. Wider public endorsement is also important.

In order to gain this broadly-based legitimacy for action, leaders and managers need to negotiate endorsement for their ambitions with stakeholders. This needs to be more than a cursory process if radical action is to be taken and defended by the stakeholders. For example it may involve negotiation with stakeholders, building support and commitment to particular courses of action with key partners, opening up strategic planning processes to significant external influence, perhaps setting up a high-profile citizens' enquiry.

Effective leaders across the system use, to a greater or lesser extent, the kind of consultative approaches promoted by public value proponents. However, it is also true that the current predominance of centralised performance management systems has meant that, across the range of public services, managers and leaders have tended to be primarily orientated towards their funders and planners rather than towards the customers they serve.

The performance of public services is judged by achievement of nationally-determined targets, irrespective of whether these reflect what their particular customers most desire or what their leaders and managers might judge to be the most efficient use of their resources. The FE system has tended to orient itself towards the LSC and the DfES for permission or authority for action rather than towards their communities and customers. The levels of centrally-driven scrutiny, planning and performance management of the system have encouraged this orientation.

The approach proposed by Moore suggests that legitimacy is earned by public services, not just by their achievement of government targets, but by their relationship with their public – their customers, citizens and stakeholders. It places the onus on leaders and managers to engage in an open and engaging process, and to be prepared to shape and educate thinking, to determine a course of action. Integral to Moore's theory is a challenge to the prevalent performance management approaches which encourage compliance and managerial approaches rather than the entrepreneurial and innovative approaches needed to maximise the impact of public services.

Public value thinking in the UK

Moore's thinking on public value has been developed and honed for the UK context. An early analysis was by the Government's Strategy Unit in the Cabinet Office[4] but the main development has been undertaken by Professor John Benington, Professor of Public Policy and Management at Warwick University and by Will Hutton and Louise Horner and team at The Work Foundation.[5]

UK proponents have argued that public value offers a potential development from New Public Management (NPM) theory which sought to bring in private sector doctrines and practices to public sector performance management in order to deal with capture of public services by public sector bodies. The theory promoted the importance of consumers rather than citizens and the numerical quantification of quality through targets. Benington and Hutton argue that public value theory brings back accountability downwards towards the customer and citizen, with a recognition that users are citizens as well as consumers. It also emphasises the importance of informed and knowledgeable citizens to give legitimacy to public services.

Benington has argued[6] that the NPM, top-down approach to performance management has run its course and that while it may have helped to address poor performance, it has failed to mobilise continuous improvement across the mass of public service providers. He argues that government needs a body of theory regarding public service reform and that public value could provide the theoretical underpinning for a new approach.

Public value thinking also has the potential in the UK to reinvigorate a public service ethos. It is a way of mobilising those who work in public institutions to be more responsive to the public and better at involving the public in the design and provision of services – reinvigorating an ethos of service to the public. It also emphasises the importance of clear vision and explicit values which are also central to a motivated workforce. While this chapter focuses on implications for organisational leaders, its potential to motivate the whole workforce to be outward-facing is powerful.

Because of the predominance of centralised performance measures in the UK, another dimension of public value that has been developed here is the notion of public value performance indicators. Will Hutton has been particularly concerned to develop measures that will reassure the Treasury that measurable outcomes are being achieved in return for public money. The Work Foundation has worked with the BBC and other public services to develop measures which give a fuller account of the outcomes achieved. Their version of the strategic triangle places a stronger emphasis on measurement, describing the dynamic as an iterative process of authorisation, measurement and creation of public value. The authorisation process of defining desirable outcomes would also establish the evaluative criteria for the measurement of public value.

The Work Foundation report also explores the concept of deliberation and how to listen to and refine the preferences of the public. This is complex territory. For example, when embarking on a process of consultation about development or changes to services, leaders need to make clear the strategic purposes, policies and priorities which legitimately limit their scope for negotiation; they need to be clear about their vision and values; and they need to be vigilant about capture by articulate self-interest, and lack of access for those with a less strident voice. Leaders may need to take tough and unpopular decisions and cannot simply move with a majority view. This is an area where the development of practice and guidelines is likely to be beneficial.

In summary, the thinking outlined above offers a number of important ideas:

- As public servants we must understand and value what the public wants and values in our services.
- As public servants we should consider that our role is to add public value.
- We need to be very clear about our purpose and values as the basis for discussion and deliberation with the public.
- We should be able to describe what we deliver in terms of how it adds to the public good. Although performance targets are a necessary tool in gaining

political authorisation, they should be balanced with a wider and more comprehensive account of outcomes.

- We need to think about how we gain legitimacy and authority for our role and purposes and be prepared to negotiate a settlement between legitimate and often conflicting demands, including those of politicians, customers, citizens and other stakeholders.
- Leaders and managers of public services should proactively engage customers, stakeholders and citizens in defining and shaping services in a process that simultaneously defines public value and helps to produce it.
- Leaders need to be prepared to educate and shape public preferences, not simply follow them.

Implications for leadership

As stated earlier, the approaches implied by public value thinking are part of leadership practice in the FE system. However, the scale of application has been limited in a period of unprecedented centrally-driven performance management. As we approach a more self-regulating and market-driven rather than plan-driven phase of development, there is a strong rationale for developing and opening up strategic processes to greater external participation and engagement in order to enhance the legitimacy and public buy-in to the services we offer.

In addition there is increasing impetus for public services to work more effectively together to address persistent inequalities such as social deprivation. Public value thinking encourages such an orientation.

Public value thinking promotes an essentially *proactive* role for the public leader. Leaders have a responsibility to *educate and shape* public opinion, understanding and awareness to maximise valuable outcomes. The approach calls for significant political acumen, and could extend the legitimate space within which public sector managers can operate and promote innovation while managing risk. It urges leaders to consider how to exploit the headroom that they have and to use their operational capacity creatively in order to take initiatives to deliver publicly-desirable outcomes.

Current systems of accountability point leaders overwhelmingly towards Whitehall *via* the LSC. *Public legitimacy* for the FE system depends on the support not just of government, but also of customers, citizens and taxpayers. Therefore leaders need to consider how to maintain accountability to the centre while building greater credibility with their community and citizenry. A stronger basis of legitimacy from their communities and citizens will arguably strengthen the strategic voice of leaders in the sector in contributing to government policy development.

The stronger *community focus* implied by public value thinking highlights the potential for leaders to make a real contribution to more effective and coherent public services in a local area. This is another way of promoting and delivering the wider benefits of learning and extending the reach of the FE system. By building coalitions of interest and working in partnership with other public services around desirable outcomes (for example in health, social services, local government regeneration strategies, and so on) we can highlight the education and training dimensions of a wide range of social outcomes, and establish our role in their delivery.

This implies that the wider outcomes achieved are a result of a deliberate and strategic decision to work in collaboration with for example local health professionals to achieve specific joint or integrated health and education outcomes. This is quite different to describing as public value outcomes, those outcomes which are a windfall product of existing practice. It is vital that we do not allow the notion of public value to be used as a flag of convenience simply to justify existing practice or provision.

The term 'joined-up government' has been a *leitmotif* of government rhetoric but has been stubbornly illusive at national policy level. It remains to be seen whether the alignment of objectives of employment and skills policy proposed by the Leitch Review of Skills will work in practice. Public value thinking suggests approaches that *join up action at local level*. A consultative, deliberative approach could be used to secure legitimacy and develop joint strategies with partners to address specific local issues which need to be co-ordinated across different public service areas.

There are substantial **challenges** in the deliberative approach promoted in public value thinking. For example, for the FE system, the following are likely to be particularly relevant.[7]

- Securing effective and efficient engagement with relevant policy and decision-making processes and bodies – this can be time-consuming and frustrating if there is not a reciprocal commitment to joint action, particularly if working with partners outside the FE system. Building coalitions of interest with key local partners around a clear focus or priority is a critical skill.
- Navigating complex 'authorising environments' and handling implications for governance and accountability: for example, being clear if there are lines that cannot be crossed in relation to legal requirements, equity issues, accountability or organisational policy.
- Developing organisational culture and capacity to respond to the outcomes of consultations and deliberations, including addressing aspects of the culture that get in the way of responsiveness to the public.
- Exploring the potential of public value to motivate staff and reinvigorate the sense of public service ethos.

- Managing the political sensitivities of consultation, including determining when to lead and shape public preference and when to respond.
- Readiness at different levels of the organisation, including at board level, to be publicly visible and to carry out processes in a very open manner.
- Developing capacity to deal with potential conflicts of values and priorities revealed through the processes of consultation/deliberation – this will require clarity about purpose and about any limitations to capacity to respond and must avoid raising unrealistic expectations.

The challenges above suggest the need for action research to explore effective strategies and approaches, building on current practice in order to understand how to support leaders and in developing individual, organisational and sector capacity. CEL is discussing with partners how this might be facilitated.

The analysis above suggests **questions** that leaders might ask about their approaches:

- Does the organisation play a full part within the local community of public services? Is the college or provider embedded in delivery of the learning dimension across public service delivery? Where are stronger coalitions of interest required to play a full part?
- Much current planning activity takes place behind closed doors or with the LSC. Which aspects of strategic planning might benefit particularly from greater external engagement?
- What processes are in place to secure legitimacy for services? What systems and processes are in place to engage the public in influencing and shaping services?
- Are there intransigent issues to do with levels of skills or participation in learning that would benefit from public debate and discussion to develop a coherent and robust strategy? Is there a case for developing campaigns or high-profile activities with stakeholders in order to shift patterns of participation or engagement with education and training?
- Do performance management systems in the organisation promote outward-facing and innovative thinking? Could the strategic triangle help staff at different levels of the organisation to be more innovative and to manage risk more safely?

Potential benefits

This paper argues that public value offers us a way of looking at the role of the leader of public services which orientates the focus towards taking greater agency and authority for action on the basis of clear legitimacy and public accountability and an unambiguous public service ethos and purpose. It is clearly not an entirely new way of looking at the world, but it has potential to shift priorities and could offer the benefit for the FE system of:

- enhancing legitimacy and authority;
- providing a stronger basis for self-regulation;
- building reputation with the wider public as well as with direct customers; and
- increasing its contribution to public service delivery and outcomes.

Notes

1 Mark Moore is Hauser Professor of Non-profit Organizations and Faculty Director of the Hauser Center. See http://ksgfaculty.harvard.edu/mark_moore for more info.
2 Grigg, P., Mager, C. (2005) LSDA. Available at http://www.lsneducation.org.uk/user/order.aspx?code=041940&src=XOWEB&cookie_test=true
3 Moore, M.H. (1995) *Creating Public Value: Strategic Management in Government.* Harvard University Press.
4 Kelly, G., Mulgan, G. and Muers, S. (2002) *Creating Public Value: An Analytical Framework for Public Service Reform.* Strategy Unit, Cabinet Office. Available at http://www.cabinetoffice.gov.uk/strategy/downloads/files/public_value2.pdf
5 *Public Value – Deliberative Democracy and the Role of Public Managers,* Louise Horner, Rohit Lekhi and Ricardo Blaug, The Work Foundation, November 2006. http://www.theworkfoundation.com/Assets/PDFs/PVfinal_report_AG.pdf
6 See the notes of the CEL policy seminar with John Benington at http://www.centreforexcellence.org.uk/UsersDoc/SeminarTwoProgrammeNotes.pdf
7 Adapted from a presentation by Louise Horner, The Work Foundation.

CHAPTER 9

Five tests for Leitch
Duncan O'Leary

Introduction

The publication of the Leitch Review of skills marked an important moment in the political trajectory of adult skills. Rather like the Stern Report on climate change, the Leitch report illustrated starkly the costs associated with *failing* to address a vital, long-term challenge for Britain.

The public value of learning was framed in economic terms, with a concern for social outcomes.[1] In a globalised world, the report argued, we need the politics of 'and': social justice *and* economic success going hand-in-hand; economic performance *and* social inclusion inextricably linked. World-class skills were framed as a neccessity, not a choice.

Much of this ambition is welcome. Progressive economic and social goals depend in large part on addressing Britain's skills deficit. And a responsive system of training provision is a prerequisite.

Yet the debate about what these goals mean in practice is far from over – largely because the Leitch ambitions risk being undermined by a damaging paradox. Whilst maximising the talents of the whole population matters *more than ever* in creating economic and social success, the danger is that skills formation becomes a source of greater *polarisation* rather than an antidote to it. The paradox is that participation currently happens in inverse proportion to need – those with the lowest skill levels are also the least likely to benefit from education and training:

- only 52 per cent of those with basic skills difficulties take part in learning compared to 83 per cent of those without;[2]
- less than one-third of adults with no qualifications participate in learning compared to 94 per cent of those with at least Level 4 qualifications;[3]
- people without qualifications are three times less likely to receive job-related training compared with those with some qualifications.[4]

To achieve the Leitch ambitions, Britian must first overcome this paradox. This chapter assesses the likelihood that the analysis and recommendations put forward in the Leitch report will achieve this goal. In particular, it tests five key assumptions that underpin the analysis in the report, with a view to exploring a wider set of issues at play.

The chapter addresses each of these tests in turn, before closing with a series of policy options, which are designed to provoke debate. Demos intends to interrogate, explore and expand on these ideas as part of a year-long study into the causes and possible solutions to Britain's skills paradox.

Test 1: are the interests of individual employers and the needs of the economy and wider society the same – and should public policy treat them as so?

> 'The skills system must meet the needs of individuals and employers. Vocational skills must be demand-led rather than centrally planned'.
> – Leitch Review final report

Employers are mentioned over 700 times in the Leitch report, often in the same sentence as individuals and wider society. The implicit message of the report is that the needs of all three are either the same thing, or can at least be reconciled with one another in a 'demand-led' system.

The question left unanswered by the report, however, is how policy should cope with potential conflicts in this triumvirate. Are the interests of employers and wider society identical, or just overlapping? If they come into conflict with one another, where should agency lie within the system?

The logic of market failure is that the (aggregated) needs of individual employers and the needs of *the economy* are often not the same thing. Employers want highly-skilled employees, but would prefer competitors to withstand the costs of that training.

In this context, the ability of government to facilitate collective decision-making is vital. Yet whilst this provides the rationale for much of the public spending recommended in the Leitch Review, the potential divergence between aggregated individual interests and the collective choices that we might take as a society is not explored fully.

A key element of this is that while a qualification to an individual worker may be his or her passport to another job, to an employer it may be a wasted investment and a way to boost the competition. For this reason, there are conflicts between social goals and individual choices – not just where levels of investment are concerned, but also in *how money is spent*. Employers are always likely to invest in job-specific – or at least company-specific – training, rather than the kind of learning and qualifications that will empower employees to take up new and different opportunities in the labour market.[5] Agency becomes vital – particularly when tax-payers' money is being spent.

None of this is to question the ethics or values of employers – or their legitimate role as a stakeholder in public policy – but, rather, to identify that perfectly rational decisions can be made in markets that lead to outcomes that no-one is happy with. Even a policy framed in economic terms, therefore, must distinguish between the public value aspired to through social policy and the aggregated private value of the distributed decisions made in a market.

Test 2: does the evidence show a universal ambition among employers to move up the value chain?

Building a demand-led system is the only way in which to increase employer and individual investment in skills and ensure that increased investment delivers economically valuable skills.

– Leitch Review final report

Closely linked to the need to separate the choices made by individual employers and the goals of social policy is the question of whether all employers actually *want or need* a highly-skilled workforce. There is good evidence to show a correlation between high skills and high performance,[6] but does it follow that *all* employers want to pursue business models based on high-value added when other approaches may be both profitable and less risk-laden?

One of underpinning principles of the Leitch Review is that a (reformed) education and training system will ensure that demand for skills from both individuals and employers is not suppressed in the future. A responsive system, it implies, will unleash demand.

However, whilst the need for a responsive system is self-evident, it is far from clear that a more responsive system will itself bring about significant increases in the *demand* for skills among employers over the long-term. The Leitch Review argues that 'Train to Gain' has been a success in this respect – helping employers to understand their own needs and providing high-class tailored provision.

The popularity of the programme among those involved with it is clear, but the likelihood of the programme realising its goals is not. The final evaluation of the Employer Training Pilots found that 'estimates would suggest about 10 per cent to 15 per cent of the training is additional training, and about 85 per cent to 90 per cent is deadweight'.[7]

This reflects the reality that many employers – entirely understandably – continue to pursue low-end product strategies which require relatively little skills development for employees, whether that development is funded by the State or not. Funding may be available, but if there is a fundamental absence of demand for higher skills among individual employers then take-up is always likely to be limited. The difficulty with voluntary, entitlement-based policies, therefore, is that they risk subsidising existing training rather than creating more of it.

A key question is whether there are other ways in which government can help shift the UK economy up the value chain, boosting overall demand for skills without losing the high levels of employment seen in recent years. Should policy-makers decide the answer to this question is 'yes', then a more assertive labour market policy becomes an option – designed to shift employers' business models up the value chain faster and further than an unregulated market would do on its own. Conversely, a decision that this is too risky still raises some important issues: if some employers are *never* likely to invest in the skills of their employees under present arrangements, then government must assess how it can kick-start social mobility by providing access to training for employees in these firms.

Test 3: does the evidence show that all individuals make decisions on long-term, economic self-interest?

> *'All individuals will have a greater awareness of the value of skills development and easier access to the opportunities available'*
>
> – Leitch Review final report

A further leap of faith in the Leitch report is that all individuals want to invest time, energy and money in their own skills. The report calls for a new partnership between the State, employers and individuals, arguing that the costs of training should be shared between all three.

Both the interim and final reports present clear evidence of the returns to individuals provided by qualifications, noting that:

- only half of those people with no qualifications are in work, compared with 90 per cent of adults qualified to degree level;
- those with A-levels are paid around 15 per cent more;
- those with a degree are paid around 25 per cent more than those without.[8]

However, it is far from clear that entitlements to Level 2 qualifications and information alone will create motivation for *individuals* if there are wider reasons preventing people from learning.

At present, there is a significant group of people who, when asked, express no desire to participate in learning. According to a recent study, half of non-learners reported that they were not interested in pursuing learning, either for personal interest or for reasons related to their current or future job or career.[9]

The same study found that 'There is really nothing one could offer the "Not at any price" cluster to encourage them to take up learning – 80 per cent say none of the incentives suggested would have any effect.'[10]

This reflects the harsh reality that, whilst training to Levels 3 and 4 may hold the *eventual* promise of financial return, that may also seem a long way off for the 11.5 million adults currently lacking a Level 2 qualification at the moment. What seems a rational choice from the treasury may not seem quite so straightforward from another perspective.

Further to this, there is evidence to suggest that a more profound set of factors may work against seemingly 'rational' decisions. One well-publicised study in the US found that our own personal views on *the very nature of learning and intelligence* can predict (and affect) levels of participation and achievement in learning.

The study, which tracked levels of educational achievement over time, found that 'Some people believe that intelligence is a fixed trait. They have a certain amount of it and that's that. We call this an "entity theory" of intelligence because intelligence is portrayed as a entity that dwells within us and that we can't change'. Others, the study found, view intelligence as malleable – something that can be shaped and added to over time.[11] The authors' conclusion from the study was that 'entity theorists' not only make reluctant learners – but are even more likely to pass up valuable learning opportunities, whilst those who regard intelligence as malleable were far more likely to participate and progress.

Compounding the effects of these personal theories of intelligence is the well-documented problem of the persistent lack of parity between vocational and academic qualifications, and the corrosive impact this has on the motivations and attitudes of distinct groups of learners in our system. There is not sufficient space to review that debate here, but what is clear is that if learning is seen only in instrumental terms, then the absence of clear benefits is still more likely to dampen any nascent desire to learn.

Test 4: in what ways do personal and social circumstances affect the ability of employers and individuals to take up opportunities to train, even when they are provided in an entitlement?

'An individual can use their Learner Account to act on the advice of the new national careers service. They will find out in advance what their financial support entitlement is, helping them to make an informed decision about the type and length of course they undertake. People will be more in control of their learning.'

– Leitch Review

Just as businesses and individuals frame their self-interest in different ways, our ability to act on our aspirations and preferences can also be stifled or supported by a wide range of factors.

Much economics is predicated on the existence of rational economic man (*sic*), but the complexity of our everyday lives – whether in organisations, communities, or families – mitigates the choices that look inevitable in a macro-economic model created in Whitehall. A key question is not just what people *perceive* to be their own rational self-interest, but what is *possible* in practice.

Three clear examples of this are:

1. Small businesses
   Investment in skills over time requires sufficient capital and resilience in companies to ensure that they can pay for training and cope with short-term losses in productive capacity. These are not always characteristics of small and medium-sized enterprises (SMEs), however, which often cannot draw on the economies of scale available to larger enterprises. This is a particular challenge, given that 50 per cent of workers with less than Level 2 attainment work for firms with fewer than 50 employees.[12]
2. Families
   Families are mentioned only three times in the Leitch report, but most of us are part of one – and many of us have caring responsibilities. Seventy per cent of couples with dependent children are now both in work,[13] and with an ageing population, many people are increasingly finding themselves part of the 'sandwich generation' – with responsibilities to care for their parents *and* children. Such commitments can mean that finance is not the only scarce resource preventing participation in education and training – time is too.
3. Older workers
   Research published by the Department for Trade and Industry has shown that older workers not only start at a disadvantage (holding fewer qualifications), but also train less than younger counterparts. And, equally worryingly, their participation levels are dipping.[14] This raises questions as to where funding can best be targeted. It may be that those with the greatest number of dependants are also those most likely to require some financial support from the State – when public money has often been targeted at those much younger.

   Leitch, of course, does recognise the role that personal and social circumstances can play, highlighting concerns over social mobility and the importance of mechanisms such as the Adult Learning Grant. However, the wider set of issues in play, from business size to family make-up, illustrate the importance of addressing the full range of barriers that prevent people taking up learning opportunities.

Test 5: are there no value-based decisions to be made in skills policy?

> *'Establishing the employer-led Commission will help to 'depoliticise' the skills agenda by securing a broad political and stakeholder consensus for the UK's world-class ambitions for 2020 and beyond.'*
>
> – Leitch Review

It has become axiomatic to argue that economic competitiveness and social inclusion are two sides of the same coin: improve one and you can improve the other; the weakness of one is a constraint on the other. The politics of 'and' – in rhetoric at least – is fast becoming part of a cross-party consensus. Soon after his election as leader of the Conservative party, David Cameron argued in a speech to Demos, '"Social justice and economic efficiency" are the common ground of British politics'.[15]

This widespread acceptance of the politics of 'and' is in part political, but it also stems from some success in halting or reversing a number of trends towards poverty and wider inequality in recent years. A comprehensive report by the independent Equalities Review showed significant progress over the last ten years, relative to the sharp growth in overall income and wealth inequality during the 1980s, for example.[16]

However, examination of the evidence on a whole variety of areas suggests that reality is more complicated than a simple synergy of economic and social goals. In spite of a decade of growth in Britain, levels of poverty remain high.[17] Inter-generational social mobility has slowed, and is lower in Britain than most Northern European countries.[18]

In this sense, the insight that a strong economy can support social goals should not be confused with the impression that there are *no* trade-offs in policy in this area. This means that policy-makers will need to separate the social and the economic conceptually and, in some cases, in policy terms. And as Leitch demonstrated in his interim report, there are important *political* decisions to be made around where investment should be targeted in the future.

This raises some important issues: that political leadership – not just economic analysis – will be needed to take important, values-based decisions in the future. And that, on this basis, the suggestion in the Review that skills policy needs to be 'depoliticised', along the lines of interest rates, looks flawed. A skills commission to 'take the politics out' of skills policy seems likely to simply outsource the politics – deliberation around value-based decisions – to an unelected body, unless politicians maintain the primary responsibility for setting the overall goals for the system.

Conclusion

The implication of the analysis put forward in this paper is that, whilst the Leitch ambition is welcome, a more creative and politically brave approach will be required to achieve it in practice. The Leitch analysis rests on a number of important assumptions – notably the five areas examined in this chapter – and the evidence calls each of those assumptions into question.

This suggests that a number of areas of policy will need revisiting. Key areas for discussion look to be:

Revisiting the Tomlinson proposals

It must be asked whether the Leitch ambition can be achieved without the Tomlinson recommendations. It is hard to see how a skills policy can operate well without changes to the education system that underlies it. As the British Chamber of Commerce's Skills Taskforce argued, 'The economy requires young people who are educated *and* trained not educated *or* trained.'[19] (our emphasis)

Defining where agency lies in a 'demand-led' system

The years until 2010 will provide a key test as to whether a system based on entitlements for firms is ever likely to succeed in confronting the skills paradox. The analysis presented in this chapter suggests that it will not. History shows that market outcomes are skewed towards those already well-endowed, indicating that even if there is an upsurge in the overall level of training, the paradox we have described may persist. A 'post-voluntary system', as described by the Chancellor, built upon entitlements for individuals, may well be needed to ensure that investment (and time) are available to all.

Exploring the balance between national entitlements and local innovation

Universal entitlements are one of the central tenets of the welfare state and the role of central government in guaranteeing equity is vital. In addition to this, however, scope for local innovation may be crucial if the myriad of wider barriers preventing people from participating are to be addressed. Put simply, the needs of working mothers in Newcastle require a different response to Baby-Boomers contemplating part-time work in Devon. As Ken Spours and colleagues at the Institute of Education have indicated,[20] this may mean finding a new balance, over the long-term, between national entitlements and local innovation.

Distinguishing between outcome-based policies and measuring activity

One of the most controversial elements of the Leitch report is the suggestion that the national education and training system should deliver more economically valuable skills, by allowing public funding only for qualifications approved by SSCs. At first glance, this appears to be an outcome-focused model of funding, rewarding training that has a recognisable (and economically valuable) end product.

This raises two sets of questions:

First, who within the system is best placed to identify which qualifications are 'economically valuable'? As Mick Fletcher has written, 'individuals and employers will be able to choose only if they want what the government thinks is good for them. . .what is also going on is a move away from a system in which local LSC staff negotiated an appropriate balance between national, regional and sectoral priorities and the realities of local demand described in college plans; and towards a system in which the mandarins and their surrogates in SSCs make whole categories of provision and people ineligible for public funding'.[21]

Second, the Leitch model measures and funds *activity* – what someone is studying at any one time – rather than providing money in exchange for outcomes. Therefore, a key question is whether, even if it is accepted that the desired outcome is an accredited qualification, it follows that government should only fund activity directly linked to that qualification. Will an overly rationalistic model of funding have the unintended consequence of reducing the participation of the very people who need it the most? Is there scope for a more decentralised system that maintains qualifications of some description as the overall goal of the system, but does not prescribe how that is achieved for the money available?

Rethinking incentives for business to move up the value chain

Governments make markets – and can remake 'self-interest'. A key question for the future is how could the Government imaginatively recast the market incentives around training for individuals and organisations? To date there has been little new thinking on how best to incentivise individuals and organisations whether through tax breaks or other imaginative inducements. Leitch has already been criticised for a lack of imagination in this area.[22]

Experimenting with the role of peer-to-peer relationships

Peer-to-peer relationships can be extremely important in helping establish a culture that either reveres learning and its benefits, or resents it. The success of union learning representatives is testament to this. Further, businesses across the country are beginning to recognise the value of peer-to-peer relationships from social software on the internet,[23] to 'buzz marketing'[24] in the commercial world and peer-to-peer recruitment in the labour market.[25] Malcolm Gladwell describes 'tipping points' created by peer-to-peer 'epidemics' – and this may be an under-explored area in education and training policy.

A national peer-to-peer system, rewarding individuals, unions, and other intermediaries for introducing friends and colleagues to (completed) modules of adult learning might be one way of helping bring about a shift in attitudes to learning in the UK. Shouldn't we *all* be learning brokers?

Evaluating the role of the public sector

Whilst the Leitch report centres on employer needs and behaviours, it has little to say on the role of a large, nationwide employer: the public sector. The role and influence of the public sector – including the relative political centralisation of Britain – needs to be explored in more detail, particularly in the context of widening economic disparities between regions.

Building a new politics

Beyond from the specific questions relating to skills policy discussed in this chapter, there is a need for something more profound: a political debate which recognises that overlapping economic social and economic goals can still come into conflict. Social justice and economic success are neither mutually exclusive, nor the same thing. It has been argued that 'we get the politicians we deserve', through our own collective failure to embrace tough choices when faced with them.[26]

With a new political era in sight, the challenge for all parties is not just to fill in the gaps that the Leitch review left blank, but to bring an element of maturity to political debate, connecting inspiring vision with real trade-offs and choices. Public value rests on public debate. We may not like the politics of 'or', but we are going to need it.

Notes

1 The terms of reference for the review were 'to examine the UK's optimal skills mix in order to maximise economic growth, productivity and social justice'.
2 *Skills in England 2004*, Volume 1, LSC (2005)

3 DfES (2003) *National Adult Learning Survey 2002.*
4 http://www.poverty.org.uk/summary/key%20facts.shtml
5 See the study on the training of music instructors for a fascinating example of this. Contrasting two training offers, it found that: under one regime, training expands horizons and develops abilities, while under the second, instructors are taught to conform and follow scripts written by others. [*Learning as Work: Teaching and learning processes in contemporary work organisations*, University of Cardiff (2006)]
6 Treasury Skills and productivity
7 DfES (2005) *The Impact of the Employer Training Pilots on the Take-up of Training Among Employers and Employees.*
8 Leitch Review interim report, HM Treasury (2005)
9 LSDA (2005) *Paying for Learning Study: Learners, Tuition Fees and the New Skills Strategy.*
10 LSDA (2005) *Paying for Learning Study: Learners, Tuition Fees and the New Skills Strategy.*
11 Dweck, C. (2000) 'Self-theories: Their Role in Motivation, Personality, and Development', *Psychology Press*, 1 edition (January 1, 2000)
12 Cabinet Office (2001) *In Demand.*
13 Demos (2006) *The Other Glass Ceiling.*
14 Unwin, P. *Age Matters: A Review of Existing Suvey Evidence.* DTI.
15 Cameron, D. speech to Demos, 'Modern Conservatism', January 2005
16 *Freedom and Fairness: The final report of the equalities review* (2007)
17 Institute for Fiscal Studies (2005) *Poverty and Inequality in Britain.*
18 Centre for Economic Performance (2005) *Intergenerational Mobility in Europe and North America.* LSE.
19 *Skills in Business*, Report of The British Chambers of Commerce Skills Taskforce, (2004)
20 Spours, K. (forthcoming) *The New Localism and Strategies for Democractic Renewal: Implications for the Governance of Inclusive Local Learning Systems.*
21 Fletcher, M. 'Choose any course, as long as it's this one', *Education Guardian*, 6 February, 2007.
22 Conservative Policy Review (2006) *Elevating the Practical.*
23 O'Reilly, T. What is Web 2.0, (http://www.oreillynet.com/pub/a/oreilly/tim/news/2005/09/30/what-is-web-20.html
24 Rosen, E. (2000) *The Anatomy of Buzz: How to Create a Word-of-mouth Marketing.*
25 See 'Can Britain produce a success like Youtube?', *Technology Guardian*, 16 October 2006 or www.zubka.com
26 Bentley, T. (2006) *Everyday Democracy: Why We Get the Politicians We Deserve*, Demos.

CHAPTER 10

Learners' perspectives

RICHARD BOLSIN

Public opinion and policy

Prevailing attitudes to the public value of adult learning are at best ambivalent. A survey undertaken by the National Institute for Adult Continuing Education (NIACE) in 2006 showed that barely 50 per cent of adults questioned believed that the taxpayer or the government should subsidise lifelong learning. One member of the public e-mailing a BBC website discussing cuts in funding for adult education classes dismissed it as:

> '...very expensive, and of little real value. Any drop in the numbers staying on should be welcomed. It would be great if it fell to zero. School leavers should all get jobs. Training is the brainchild of politicians with Jurassic attitudes.'

Another reflected scepticism about traditional attitudes to lifelong learning:

> 'It depends how you look at the figures. There's a decline in people watching mass market TV like the BBC, but more people are watching TV, they're just getting it from new sources such as YouTube which you could call niche TV. The same goes for adult education. Fewer people are taking part with the established providers, but more people overall could be involved in adult education, just accessing it from millions of new sources. As a result, adult education should become more productive.'

In the face of such evidence, and in the knowledge that funding for discretionary services like lifelong learning will always take second place to spending on schools and universities, should we be surprised by government policy or the advice offered by Lord Leitch and others?

Human instinct and intelligence

Evidence consistently emerging from research over the last 20 years on the workings of the human brain has led us to reappraise fundamentally our understanding of human instinct and intelligence.

We know that healthy humans are born equally with three instincts or impulses:

- to breathe;
- to feed (initially through a reflex to suck); and
- to learn.

Without any of those three instincts life would end, or at the very least be seriously impaired. What's more, those impulses remain with us for life, each equally vital, life-saving, life-transforming, life-long. And for adults, our quality of life is conditioned by the extent to which we continue to learn, whether for pleasure or gain. It is also a significant factor in the extent to which humans are able to improve the quality of life for others, whether they act as 'radiators' or 'drains', adding public value, or by being dependent, detracting from it.

In the 1980s, Howard Gardner, a professor of psychology at Harvard, developed a theory of multiple intelligence in humans. This has become increasingly accepted and adopted by educators, especially in schools, as fundamental to understanding and enabling children in particular to learn successfully. Gardner identifies at least nine human intelligences:

- linguistic (reading, writing, speaking, listening);
- logical-mathematical (numeracy);
- spatial (the intelligence needed by architects, sculptors, and so on);
- bodily-kinaesthetic (the intelligence needed by dancers, athletes, and so on);
- musical;
- interpersonal (ability to engage effectively with others);
- intrapersonal (ability to understand self, emotional intelligence);
- naturalist (understanding the natural environment); and
- existential (understanding 'big ideas').

Our school system recognises the first two of these well in assessing pupil performance to the age of 14. Yet there is compelling evidence that functional adults also need a high level of interpersonal and intrapersonal intelligence to be effective socially or at work; and to understand the profile they have in the remaining intelligences to enjoy or improve their quality of life. It requires intelligence and appreciation to listen to music, for instance, as well as to play an instrument, and the same applies to bodily-kinaesthetic intelligence and sport.

Theories like these increasingly begin to question assumptions on which our education systems, policy and institutions have been founded. Quality of life and the potential to improve it for oneself or others depends significantly on the ability to learn throughout life.

The public value of adult learning

These findings are supported in a different way by the Learning and Skills Development Agency (LSDA) research on the benefits of adult education. This found that adults through learning increased their:

- self-confidence and esteem;
- independent thinking;
- problem-solving;
- employability;
- IT skills;
- social integration;
- mental and physical health and family life;
- quality of life; and
- positive attitudes.

We know that confident adults help to grow confident, successful families and communities; that independent thinking promotes research skills, critical thinking, enterprise, innovation and creativity; that improved mental and physical health reduces the risk of dependency and the cost of third party interventions; and that successful communities sustain themselves by attracting inward investment, improving safety and quality of life and by creating conditions in which a strong voluntary sector can also flourish.

Examples of successful adult learning add considerable weight to the evidence that adult learning adds to public value. This evidence is often hard to demonstrate statistically, although we must continue to endeavour to find ways to do so. Often the most valuable and compelling evidence of the value of adult education comes from individual learner histories.

Reach Out

Mike Buchan was a recovering alcoholic undergoing cancer treatment when he joined a Workers' Educational Association (WEA) Reach Out course in January 2004. Reach Out is a project in Aberdeen for unemployed adults who are marginalised in society because of any of a range of barriers – including disability, mental health problems and alcohol or substance misuse. Through Reach Out, Mike was able to go on courses in subjects including literacy, outdoor and environmental education, health promotion and the arts. He has now developed a previous interest in hill-walking and hopes to qualify soon as a climbing instructor and mountain leader trainer. He has also become active as a spokesperson and volunteer for the project.

'I've learned a great many things and relearned skills I already had. Now I know how to use my skills and to just be me. Before, I was really lacking in confidence, I found it difficult to speak to folk and deal with life. Now I've learned to trust and that's been the hardest part. Without Reach Out, I don't think I would have survived.'

Swans

Sometimes We All Need Support (SWANS) is a centre for disabled adults in Maldon, Essex. It provides a safe place where its members can go in order to learn a new skill or enjoy a therapeutic pastime. In the last two years the WEA has provided tutors for up to 15 different courses per week at SWANS. Subjects offered to members include arts, computer skills, cookery, financial planning and an accredited course to become a teaching assistant. The courses have been popular as they are based on what SWANS members want to learn, rather than 'off-the-shelf' courses. Other education providers had proved unable to provide this flexible response to the needs of the centre's members. Julia Dowling, the Manager of SWANS and herself disabled, says:

'I can honestly say with utter conviction that SWANS members have had life-changing experiences as a result of WEA involvement. Some have gone on to work and others have been eased into independent living.'

Tandrusti[1]

A WEA project in Dudley has addressed social barriers faced by older members of South Asian communities by providing health and fitness courses. Most Tandrusti courses are different to typical 'keep fit' classes – for instance, there is a community gym and a running club for the over-70s, with the involvement of project patron Fauja Singh, who is 94 and holds the world record for the marathon in the over-90 age category. Many of the courses are designed to help with specific medical issues – such as cardiac rehabilitation or postural stability (helping to prevent falling).

The courses lead directly to health benefits including reduced blood pressure: 98 per cent of students surveyed showed a significant reduction. Students say that the project also enables them to meet more people and improves their sense of wellbeing. The project has close links with a wide range of community organisations in Dudley representing the Sikh, Hindu, Muslim, Bangladeshi, African-Caribbean and Yemeni communities, thereby also breaking down other barriers and contributing to community cohesion.

Attendance on a Tandrusti course has been the starting point for many students on a 'learning journey' into other forms of education and into volunteering. Volunteers help with translation, word-of-mouth recruitment and course organisation – and some have gone on to become mentors or tutors. Language and cultural awareness training is given to tutors and volunteers when needed, and appropriate venues and dress codes are used. An independent review of the Tandrusti project in February 2004 said:

> *'The Tandrusti project has had a demonstrable impact on developing the capacity of people within Dudley's South Asian communities to become involved in training and volunteering activities.'*

Helping in Schools

Helping in Schools (HiS) is a well-established WEA programme enabling over 1,800 parents each year to develop skills and knowledge to become volunteers in primary schools. It is highly valued by schools and head-teachers and is delivered in educationally-disadvantaged areas. It has multiple outcomes and learning levels. As well as engaging parents with schools, encouraging children to value their education and developing Parent-Teacher Associations and new school governors, HiS has impressive outcomes for students in terms of employment within schools and progression to other education and training.

The prime target group for the course is adults who left school with few or no qualifications, as illustrated in the table below.

Students	2002/3	2003/4	2004/5	2005/6
No known qualification	8.7%	8.3%	11.1%	10.8%
Level 1 qualification	10.9%	18.8%	19.7%	20.8%
Level 2/3 qualification	46.3%	44.1%	39.0%	36.0%
Level 4/5 qualification	11.9%	13.4%	10.9%	15.53%
Proportion from disadvantaged postcodes	25.5%	30.1%	35.5%	31.9%
Declared ethnic minority	11.4%	13.6%	17.7%	17.9%

Since 1999 the WEA has conducted an annual postal survey of subsequent destinations of the Helping in Schools students who had enrolled in the previous academic year. These surveys have produced a response rate of 38-51 per cent of those who completed the course. A summary of these surveys is given below.

Survey year	2001	2002	2003	2004	2005	2006
Still school volunteer	25.1%	42.5%	40.8%	43.1%	36.9%	41.0%
School governor	8.2%	4.6%	4.1%	5.9%	5.8%	4.7%
Further courses	43.6%	40.3%	37.1%	42.2%	38.6%	41.1%
Education employment	44.0%	50.8%	46.8%	53.4%	48.2%	47.4%
Other employment	8.2%	9.8%	5.7%	4.6%	6.1%	4.3%

Rochdale Asian Women's Project

In Rochdale the WEA works to develop the language skills and confidence of Asian women, many of whom have arrived in the community through arranged marriages with limited skills for living in this country, yet with responsibility for looking after large extended families. The starting point for many women is sewing and embroidery, which builds on skills which are transferable from their previous environments. This merely serves as a springboard for them to gain employment and further qualifications, which include becoming tutors for the Project. This is what they say:

'I first became interested in the WEA through a friend and enrolled onto digital embroidery, IT and sewing. I was helped to apply for a loan from the Prince's Trust. I used the loan to open my own business, a clothing boutique called "Unique". Due to its success I won the award for Asian Business of the Year in Rochdale. A big thanks to the WEA for giving me the confidence to start my own business.'

Shafqat Parveen

'The main reason for enrolling on my course (digital embroidery) was my deflated confidence and low self-esteem. I soon realised that the environment in the classroom was very welcoming and it attracted me to courses like IT. I had already graduated in beauty and used the confidence I gained from attending WEA courses to my advantage. I found the strength to go ahead and open my mobile beauty salon. I am proud to say that now I can make use of my skills all thanks to the WEA and recommend the courses to anyone seeking confidence or to learn further skills.'

Samina Ruffique

'I first enrolled on to an IT course and soon became interested in the other courses, ie sewing, cooking and confidence-building. I was then provided with help from Women's Enterprise to open my own business called "Spicy Caterers" and I now employ a further two employees to help me run successfully.'

Sumaira Hussain

Public value: the experience of adult learners

Students in the WEA are convinced that their participation in adult learning adds significantly to their value as citizens. The examples above demonstrate how their achievements through a very wide range of learning activity have enabled them to 'radiate' added public value (as opposed to remain in dependent, 'draining' situations). Older learners argue similarly that the energy, physical and mental, they put into learning enables them to resist disease and degeneration and add their own value to health and social services by avoiding dependency on them.

> *'The main comment I would like to make on the value of WEA courses is that these courses enable elderly people in our community to keep active minds and thus improve the quality of their lives. This aspect of adult education often seems to be overlooked. The nearest school evening classes involve driving some distance along twisting country roads in the dark, whereas the WEA courses are close to home.'*

WEA students accept the case made by the Government and its advisers like Lord Leitch to invest in improving the skills of the workforce. They understand that this inevitably leads to some learners paying higher fees for non-priority courses.

But in that case, they strongly resist and resent the levels of red-tape and bureaucracy which are applied to them, especially if their courses are not seen as important and they are meeting an increasingly large proportion of the cost themselves. Despite being assured of the cuts being made in the Learning and Skills Council and inspectorates, they see no evidence of those savings benefiting students like them.

They experience a system which is designed for full-time students aged 16 to 19, who pay no fees, being applied to older people with diverse learning objectives and more time constraints attending part-time courses. The not insignificant transactional costs of such a system are borne by them, too. How can they fail to conclude that they are not at the centre, not respected and treated simply as outputs in a system which 'farms' learning aims and qualifications and disapproves of lifelong learning?

They are also concerned and beginning to see evidence that as a result of fee increases, their classes are at risk of becoming the preserve of those with wealth. Age discrimination legislation has denied pensioners the right to a subsidy, and working people without surplus income are unable to afford the increasing cost of adult education like that illustrated above. Those costs are also deterring some partners, like schools, from participating.

WEA students believe that opportunities for serious education should be open to all, and lifelong learning for its own sake should be accessible and

Different attitudes

When my mother-in-law retired she did a short course which inspired her to do two degrees both in social sciences. But the benefit goes beyond herself, we like to argue politics etc. but having an educated opinion puts a new perspective on everything we choose to discuss, in short it opens up our minds further by listening to her. So not only do her children benefit, so will her grandchildren. Which is why I think even short courses in any subject are valuable, if they lead to that one person going on to study higher that benefit does get passed on to others as above.

Dawney, Wirral, Cheshire

Different attitudes

I have revised my French, learned modern Greek, local history, archaeology but craft classes are very restricted and all the courses I took are university-based, although not all were university level. I meet people, keep my brain active, enjoy learning. These activities reduce isolation, reduce depression and stimulate brain activity (supposed to stave off Alzheimers) so they could be a good social investment at all academic levels.

Ros, Renfrewshire

Different attitudes

I agree that it is important to encourage 16–19-year-olds to continue their education but I cannot emphasise the positive impact it has on children most vulnerable to doing poorly at school to have a parent, who perhaps also didn't do well, go back to education and re-train or enter the workforce or HE for the first time. It is more motivating to see their mum gain the confidence to become a nurse or a social worker and go to uni than to increase the funding for the 16–19-year-olds but have them see their unskilled parents struggle on.

Adult education is more than just flower arranging, it is about increasing social capital, increasing self-esteem and creating an inclusive society, this will benefit everyone, not just the fickle labour market.

Elizabeth Hanna, London

Different attitudes

…on all our courses there is always someone who needs a lift in life. Many of our students say they come to WEA courses because they are different from other local courses. They are said to be more welcoming, user friendly for all levels of ability, often they contain an element of socialisation that is missing from the courses of other providers.

WEA learner

Different attitudes

The local WEA branch put on a music course in conjunction with the University of Sussex which I attended and led to me doing a music certificate and Open University courses to gain the right ingredients to pursue my business. I now teach violin and run a group of 20 musicians who play for charity events and have taken part in cultural exchanges to France.

WEA learner

Different attitudes

We have a disabled member who regularly attends our courses. Our committee members collect her from her house, helping her to lock up, and drive her to the course venue. She is driven home again, checking that she has access to her walking aid once indoors and that her door is locked.

WEA Branch Committee Member

---

affordable to all adults. They ask where the public value lies in such circumstances.

WEA students therefore want the Government to:

- **respect** adults;
- value **multiple outcomes** of learning;
- value **knowledge** in adult learning as well as skills; and
- respect and support **individuals** as well as employers.

They would like to see:

- more 'public value';
- much less bureaucracy and regulation, especially for non-priority provision; and
- more cross-subsidy around health, regeneration and citizenship.

Conclusion

In considering the learner's perspective of public value in adult education, I have so far avoided reference to the theory developed by Professor Mark Moore at Harvard University and Professor John Benington at Warwick University as a framework through which to analyse and develop the role of leaders in creating outcomes that are considered desirable by the public. The theory requires leaders to apply and evaluate public value through a triangular strategic framework which takes account of:

- the **authorising or political environment** – ensuring that customers, stakeholders, sponsors and funders support the proposed action;
- the **operational capacity** – ensuring that the organisation has the operational capacity, skills and competences to carry out the proposed action; and
- **public value strategic goals** – ensuring that the action is in line with the values, mission and purpose of the organisation.

It is clear that these three factors are also present in the examples above. The authorising environment is created through partnerships with other organisations representing the students. Often, successful bids for funding further strengthen that authorisation. Schools, universities and higher education providers health trusts and local councils add further authority, and some projects benefit from high-profile champions and patrons. Operational capacity is also evident, particularly in the frequency with which students become tutors themselves (as in Reach Out, Helping in Schools and the Rochdale Women's Project). In the case of the WEA, the examples referred to above result not from high-level strategic planning decisions which are then transmitted through the organisation, but from the imagination, commitment and effectiveness of frontline organisers working in the heart of local communities, exploiting opportunities which present themselves. This is very much in keeping with the mission and purpose of the WEA, and its practice of starting with the needs of individuals rather than the need to fill classrooms or apply a particular curriculum or product.

Public value is therefore alive and kicking in adult education, even if it appears to remain unrecognised by prevailing attitudes, systems and policy.

Note

1 Tandrusti (Tan-drust-ee) is a sound condition of the mind or body, a state of being free from illness. A person who is 'tandrust' has good health or is capable of producing good health.

CHAPTER 11

Social justice and public value in adult learning

NICK PEARCE, SIMON BEER AND JENNY WILLIAMS

Introduction

This paper explores the public value of adult learning through the lens of social justice. It begins with the assertion that social justice is one of the shared values that, as a society, we aspire to. It then considers the implications for our education system and adult learning. The basis of this paper is a presentation entitled 'Social Justice and Adult Learning' given by Nick Pearce, at that time Director of ippr, to a NIACE/LSN seminar on the public value of adult learning in February 2007.

Tom Schuller's chapter in this volume offers three dimensions of public value in education.[1] Firstly, publicly shared beliefs or norms of a general kind, for example, in the importance of a tolerant society but one with clearly defined common values. Secondly, desirable, or valued, features or goals of the education system that would support those general beliefs. Thirdly, value judgements about the best ways of achieving those goals. The structure of Nick Pearce's presentation clearly reflected the Schuller outline.

Pearce's starting point is the four principles of social justice, set out by David Miller (2006)[2], based on the Report of the Commission on Social Justice (1994).[3] Pearce sets out elements of the research base from which to consider our progress towards attaining social justice through our education system, identifies priorities for adult learning that would support the principles of social justice, and makes a series of proposals for re-casting adult learning policy in the light of these priorities.

This paper sets out Nick Pearce's argument which was later expanded in the ippr's manifesto for adult learning[4] (March 2007). It concludes with a comment about the potential for linking Tom Schuller's interpretations of public value in education with Nick Pearce's approach, rooted in the principles of social justice, to provide a conceptual framework for exploring the complexities of public value in adult learning and the implications for future adult learning policy development.

Social justice: common values?

Essentially for Pearce, the important connection between adult learning and social justice lies in social mobility. Before going on to explore the relationship between social justice and social mobility, he outlines the development of the notion of social justice, which is worth setting out here.

Pearce describes social justice as multi-dimensional but having equality at its heart. There is no single objective that defines social justice, but a series of objectives, corresponding to the different concrete goods and bads whose distribution we care about. But the core idea of social justice is contained in the following four principles (Miller 2006):

- **Equal citizenship:** Every citizen is entitled to an equal set of civil, political and social rights, including the means to exercise these rights effectively.
- **The social minimum:** All citizens must have access to resources that adequately meet their essential needs, and allow them to live a secure and dignified life in today's society.
- **Equality of opportunity:** A person's life chances, and especially their access to jobs and educational opportunities, should depend only on their own motivation and aptitudes, and not on irrelevant features such as gender, class or ethnicity.
- **Fair distribution:** Resources that do not form part of equal citizenship or the social minimum may be distributed unequally, but the distribution must reflect relevant factors such as personal desert and personal choice.

At first glance, these principles might appear undemanding in relation to current policy. But in fact, as this paper seeks to illustrate, applying these principles to the new circumstances that we face at the start of the twenty-first century – a time of significant technological, social, cultural and environmental change – reveals alternatives to the current policy priorities for adult learning.

Pearce goes on to analyse how far the UK has progressed with the social justice agenda. Britain, he argues, is no longer the 'tired, divided and failing country' the 1994 Commission on Social Justice described. The economy has experienced steady growth since 1993, employment rates have increased and registered unemployment continues to fall. Child and pensioner poverty have been reduced. The nation is healthier, living longer and experiencing far less crime than a decade ago.

However, significant challenges remain. Levels of child poverty continue to surpass those of many of our European partners and inequalities in income, wealth and wellbeing remain stubbornly high. Parental social class and ethnic background still heavily influence life chances, whilst democratic participation has fallen and political influence is polarising according to class and wealth. And midway into the first decade of a century, it is no longer possible to think about social justice without tackling challenges that reach beyond national boundaries: environmental sustainability, migration and the movement of labour, and the fight against global poverty.

Pearce identifies several key areas in his survey of the UK's position: education attainment and equity; participation at 17; labour market issues; income equality; poverty reduction and migration.

Against OECD averages, the UK shows as a high educational attainment, but low equity country. Pearce believes that 'the countries that get it right (Finland, Sweden) do not **input** entitlements, rather they **output** entitlements'.

The drop out rate at 17 still poses serious problems for the UK. The data below shows post-16 participation stalled. Post-16 participation is Britain's biggest skill gap compared to our European neighbours. It is also a major cause of falling social mobility.

The labour market is polarised and on current trends this looks set to continue. The British labour market is good at creating jobs, but less good at encouraging progression into higher-paid, higher skilled work. The UK labour market is less regulated than many of those of its EU partners. Its product markets are open and competitive and the economy is heavily service-based. But it also has a minimum wage, a new architecture of tax credits and in-work training entitlements, a socialised National Health Service and an expanding system of early years education and childcare.

Figure 11.3 shows predicted shifts in sectors in the UK Labour market by 2020. A shift away from elementary and low skilled occupations is counterbalanced by projected growth in management, professional, skilled and technical occupations. Social mobility worked in the post-war decades in the UK because changes in the occupational structure allowed the middle classes to expand dramatically. This measure of absolute mobility appears to have halted today. The emergence of our hourglass economy and the potential problems it creates in terms of progression opportunities for those who enter employment in low skill/ low waged jobs is a central concern. What is regularly predicted is an increase in managerial, professional and technical jobs requiring high-level skills being paralleled by a rise in the number of people in less well-paid personal services and sales occupations. Despite all the talk about the advent of a 'knowledge economy', 'low grade' jobs that cannot be relocated to other parts of the world will continue to exist.

Figure 11.4 shows Leitch projections for 2020, with an increased section of the labour market having Level 4 qualifications and a substantial reduction in the number of people in work with no qualifications. It is inter-

Relationship between the average performance of participating countries on the PISA reading literacy scale and the socioeconomic gap in student performance: 2000

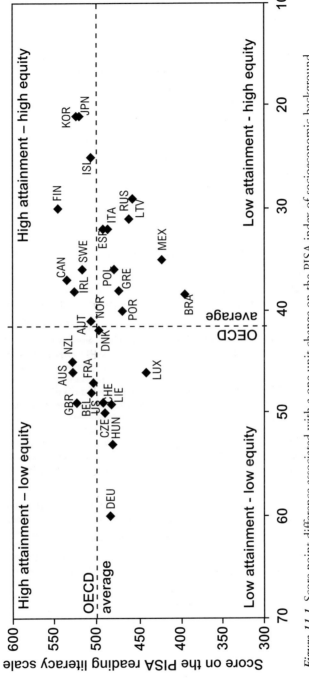

Figure 11.1 Score point difference associated with a one unit change on the PISA index of socioeconomic background
Source: DfES (2006) *Social Mobility: Narrowing Educational Social Class Attainment Gaps* 26 April 2006 London: TSO

Participation in education and training, 16-year-olds, 1950–2005

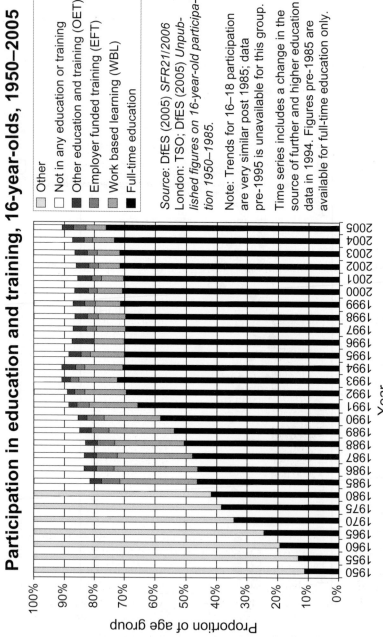

Legend:
- Other
- Not in any education or training
- Other education and training (OET)
- Employer funded training (EFT)
- Work based learning (WBL)
- Full-time education

Source: DfES (2005) *SFR21/2006* London: TSO; DfES (2005) *Unpublished figures on 16-year-old participation 1950–1985.*

Note: Trends for 16–18 participation are very similar post 1985; data pre-1995 is unavailable for this group.

Time series includes a change in the source of further and higher education data in 1994. Figures pre-1985 are available for full-time education only.

Figure 11.2

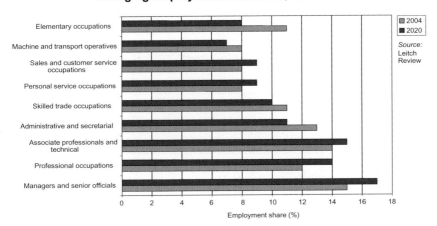

Figure 11.3

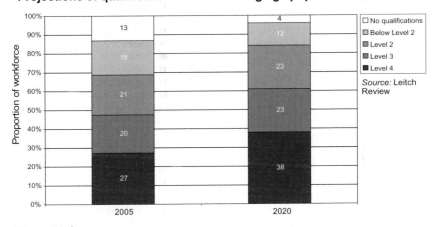

Figure 11.4

esting that Leitch and many other contributors to the debate in this area use qualifications as a proxy, rather than a broader definition of skills.

Income inequality has plateaued since 1997 (see Figure 11.5). However, wealth inequalities have grown in the 1990s and tax inequality has fallen since 1997. Perhaps more critically, income inequality has continued to rise under Labour, albeit more slowly than it did in the 1980s. This is largely due to changes at the top and bottom of the income distribution. The incomes of the top one per cent have continued to grow significantly, while those of the bottom decile have not kept pace with the average. But between these extremes, incomes have become slightly more equals.[5]

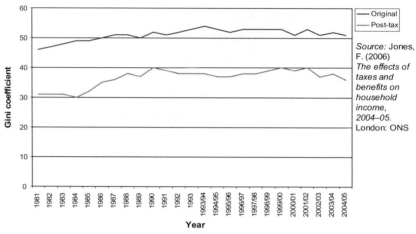

Labour market: pre and post transfers income inequality

Original and post-tax income inequality

Source: Jones, F. (2006) *The effects of taxes and benefits on household income, 2004–05.* London: ONS

Figure 11.5

When it comes to poverty reduction, there has been some progress (see Figure 11.6). Poverty has fallen since 1997 in that there is less absolute poverty. Child poverty has been reduced, partly through the impact of labour market policies. The figures for pensioners are good due to both labour policies and trend. However, for working age adults there has been no shift, so relative to the rest of society poor adults in this group have got poorer.

The last ten years has been a period of very high, but relatively concentrated, migration (Figure 11.7, Kyambi (2005) *Beyond Black and White*. London: ippr. To see interactive maps go to free access website http://news.bbc.co.uk/1/shared/spl/hi/uk/05/born_abroad/html/overview.stm). From a social justice perspective, it is an important aspect of this migration that very different immigrant experiences have been afforded. Employment rates differ greatly by nationality. As you can see in the chart below, New Zealanders and Australians enjoy 95 per cent employment whilst only 12 per cent of Somalis are in work.

Pearce's key message, in analysing the UK's social justice 'performance', is that social mobility remains 'sticky'. Elsewhere recently, ippr cited an LSE[6] study showing that the chances of an individual moving to a different income group from the one they were born into are significantly lower in Britain and the US than in more equal societies such as Canada and especially the Nordic countries. Additionally, in contrast to the US where relative intergenerational mobility has remained stable, in Britain it has fallen over time (Blanden, Gregg and Machin, 2005). In other words, people born into a manual worker family in 1970 had less chance of moving into a higher occupation than people born in similar circumstances in 1958.

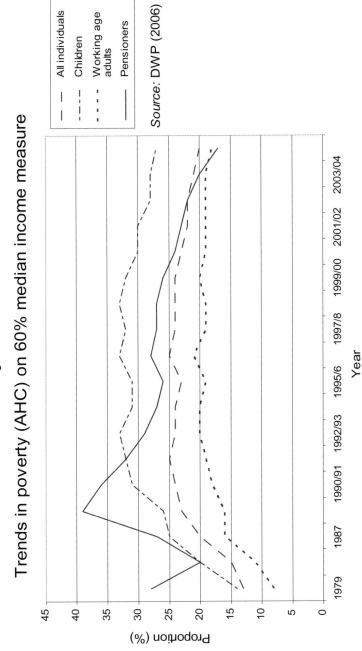

Poverty reduction

Trends in poverty (AHC) on 60% median income measure

Legend:
- – – All individuals
- – · – Children
- · · · · Working age adults
- ——— Pensioners

Source: DWP (2006)

Year

Proportion (%)

Figure 11.6

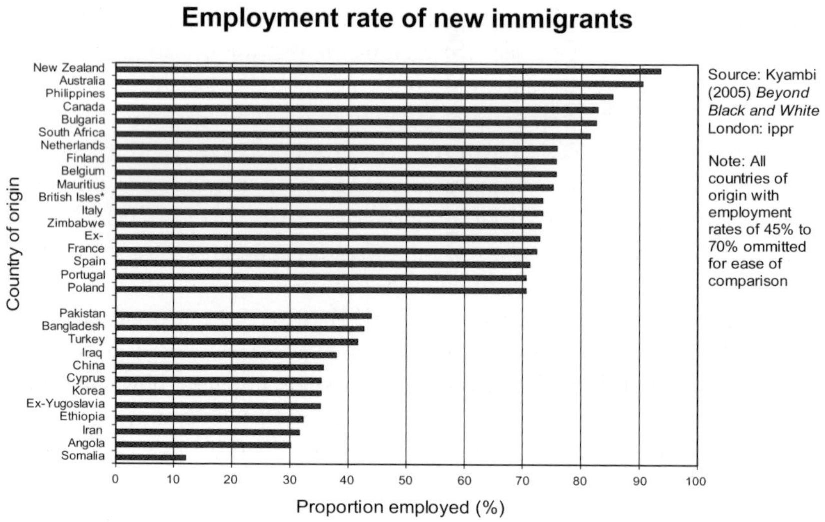

Employment rate of new immigrants

Source: Kyambi (2005) *Beyond Black and White* London: ippr

Note: All countries of origin with employment rates of 45% to 70% ommitted for ease of comparison

Figure 11.7

However, he asserts that the social justice agenda has helped forge a distinctly British model that is neither European or American. In his ippr book[7] he claims the UK better merits the title 'Anglo-Social' than Anglo-Saxon. Importantly, Pearce believes that while the UK public has little interest in European levels of equity, the concept of fairness does resonate strongly with the British public, and asks whether in some way we are 'hard wired' for fairness. For Pearce an important lesson to draw is that social justice drives social mobility, not the other way around.

A public value approach: what would it look like?

So, what should be the features of an adult learning system that supports the principles of social justice? Pearce suggests that each of the four principles of social justice can lead us towards describing the desirable features of an adult education system.

Equal citizenship should continue to be supported by a policy focus on literacy, numeracy and English for speakers of other languages (ESOL) to ensure equal civil and political liberties, as enshrined in human rights legislation.

The current policy priority around Level 2 is essentially **'the social minimum'**. However, the priority is currently cast almost entirely in relation to earning power. Within a social justice framework, the Level 2 offer should reflect wider benefits from learning and a broader sense of what we, as a society, value as a social minimum. It should, for example, reflect the impact that learning has on health and wellbeing, community safety, civic engagement and social cohesion, and a more generous interpretation of economic regeneration.

In terms of 'equality of opportunity' adults should have access to opportunities to develop their skills in order to advance their progression in the labour market. This is particularly important given the development of the UK's 'hour glass' economy which could restrict opportunities for progression for those who enter employment in low skilled/low wage jobs.

Fair distribution in adult learning that is not part of equal citizenship or the social minimum might be about learning outcomes. This is a challenging area that could form the basis of another separate paper: how should the social justice principle of fair distribution be applied so that the outcomes achieved by learners reflect their effort and choice rather than the postcode and class?

Taken individually, the application of each of the four social justice principles to adult learning seems straightforward enough. But, in the context of funding constraints for adult learning, it is arguable whether all four features of a desirable adult learning system could be kept in balance. And if it is not possible, Pearce asks, what should our priorities be? Whilst accepting the Government's identified priorities, namely Level 2 and skills for opportunity, Pearce illustrates how, by using the principles of social justice, together with what we know about both our current social justice 'performance' and what works for adult learners, a more radical framework for recasting adult learning policy might be pursued.

How to pursue the goals: implications for Adult Learning Policy

The third of Schuller's public value questions concerns how best to achieve those key features of an adult learning system that support publicly valued norms or beliefs. Here, Nick Pearce makes six proposals:

1. Start with individuals, not funders or employers.
2. Focus subsidies on priority groups and ask others to contribute towards costs.
3. Allow learners to choose what to study, certified or not.
4. Re-cast the Level 2 entitlement to make it more flexible.
5. Introduce income contingent loans for Levels 3 and 4.
6. Devolve responsibility back to local government and city regions where they exist.

Conclusion

In his paper, Schuller propounds three separate 'interpretations' of public value but taken together and posed as questions, they become three interrelated dimensions of a possible framework through which to explore the public value of adult learning.

Presenting Nick Pearce's arguments about Social Justice and Adult Learning in the way we have, clearly relates them to Tom Schuller's 'framework'. Pearce takes as his starting point the shared value of social justice, applies social justice principles to identify the desirable goals of an adult learning system that could support it, and then makes a set of proposals for re-casting adult learning policy to achieve those goals. In so doing, he makes a coherent argument for the public value of adult learning through a social justice focus. This narrative becomes a powerful case for re-thinking adult learning as a means of deploying a social justice approach geared towards achieving greater social mobility.

In the UK, achieving prosperity is now the key driver for adult learning policy. The acquisition and productive deployment of skills for employability have become mainstream policy objectives, most recently through the Leitch Review of Skills. As employment is seen as the primary route out of poverty, skills are also accorded a role in combating social exclusion and promoting greater social mobility. But in reality the relationship between economic competitiveness and social justice is more complex. If we seek social justice from investment in adult learning we may have to pursue different goals, even if they don't immediately impact on our economic competitiveness.

Taken together, the Pearce and Schuller approaches offer us a platform from which to challenge constructively the utilitarian constraints of current adult learning policy. Social justice is a theme that continues to carry purchase with policy-makers and as Pearce points out, fairness is a theme that may enable us to attain authorisation from a public with no appetite for European levels of taxation and little tradition of taking to the streets in defence of spending on adult learning.

Such a platform, in conjunction with existing efforts to engage partners and stakeholders in the design and delivery of public services and in defining their measurement frameworks, could constitute a progressive and meaningful way forward for adult learning policy. Although social justice is an important 'lens' through which to consider the public value of adult learning, there are of course others: citizenship, wider benefits of learning, and community cohesion to name but three. What we would contend, however, is that a public value/ social justice framework with a strong emphasis on understanding and helping to shape what the public wants from learning could be a starting point for a new settlement.

Notes

1 Schuller, T. (2008) Public value: International insights, this volume.
2 Miller, D. (2006) 'What is Social Justice?', in Pearce, N. and Paxton, W. (eds) *Social Justice: Building a Fairer Britain,* London: ippr.
3 Commission on Social Justice (CSJ) (1994) Social Justice: Strategies for National Renewal. London: Vintage Books.
4 Delorenzi, S. (2007) *Learning for Life: A New Framework for Adult Skills.* ippr.
5 Goodman, A., Shaw, J. and Shephard, A. (2005) 'Understanding recent trends in income inequality', in Delorenzi, S., Reed, J. and Robinson, P. (eds) *Maintaining momentum: Promoting social mobility and life chances from early years to adulthood.* London: ippr.
6 Blanden, J., Gregg, P. and Machin, S. (2005) *Intergenerational Mobility in Europe and North America.* London: LSE, Centre for Economic Performance, supported by the Sutton Trust.
7 *Social Justice*, ippr (2006).

CHAPTER 12

Conclusion

COLIN FLINT AND CHRIS HUGHES

There is an interesting paradox inherent in considering public value and adult learning. Further education colleges and adult education providers have always assumed that they were providing a service to the public, and, by and large, the public that have used their services have valued them. They have said so consistently in customer surveys, they have continued to use the services provided in large numbers. This is not to say that all perceptions of quality were uniformly high, but there were generally high levels of satisfaction.

'Public value' is a relatively new emerging framework for public management and service reform. The Work Foundation, (formerly the Industrial Society) the influential not-for-profit organisation that seeks to bring all sides of working organisations together to find the best ways of improving both economic performance and the quality of working life, offers an explanation of public value that goes like this:

> 'in contrast to traditional public administration in which public managers were responsible for meeting service targets set by politicians (e.g. a top-down bureaucratic approach) and new public management (a more market-driven approach that aimed to reduce the reach of government), public value aims to put the 'public' back in public service by placing citizens at the heart of service reform'
>
> Public Value and Learning and Skills,
> Rebecca Fauth, The Work Foundation 2007

And yet in further and adult education, the voice of the public is not heard at all, at least in areas that might influence the offer being made. The public that used to queue up to enrol for adult education classes at the beginning of the academic year is doing so in ever-declining numbers, because what they used to queue up for is becoming less and less available and more and more costly. And this, of course, is the very direct result of the iron hand of government and its agents. Educational opportunity for adults has been uncompromisingly reshaped in an attempt to get it to produce what the Government has decided is required. The public has been consulted neither before the 'reforms' were set in motion, nor since. The Government has decided what is to be public value. Citizens have not noticeably been at the heart of this reform.

This then is public value defined as that which it is believed will give most value for public money. Governments are of course entitled to make such dispositions: very large sums of money are spent on education and training, and it is entirely reasonable that strategic decisions should be made on what it is to be spent upon. Equally, those not wholly convinced by the strategy and methodologies have a right to examine some alternatives and other approaches. That is the intent of this book, the idea for which came out of the work that led to *Eight in Ten*, the report on the state of adult learning in colleges of further education in England, published by NIACE in 2005. The title referred to the fact that, at the time of the work of the independent Committee of Enquiry which NIACE had set up, eight in ten of the students enrolled in the FE system were adults. That fact was beginning to change during the period in which the Committee was meeting, and it has gone on changing ever since.

Eight in Ten endorsed the identification of the key mission of the colleges as being the provision of vocational education to adults and young people beyond the age of compulsory schooling, whilst emphasising that the colleges also contribute significantly to the achievement of other educational objectives, as in their work in general and in higher education. However, the Report stated strongly that members of the Committee believed that there were three key themes in the work that colleges undertake with adults, and that it was vital that all three themes remained central to their mission. The themes bear repeating:

- access to employability;
- workforce development;
- the creating and sustaining of cultural value.

The full definitions of these themes is to be found in the first chapter of *Eight in Ten*, entitled 'A new vision', but some of what was written about the third theme is appropriate here:

> '... providing learning opportunities that foster a critical and informed engagement with social, political and moral issues, and thus support the development of a tolerant participative democracy for all citizens and communities: that encourage appreciation and participation in the arts, sport and cultural activities: and that secure the role learning can play in the achievement of public and collective good.'

In September 2006 the first in a planned series of seminars was held by NIACE, delivered to an invited audience, under the general title of The Public Value of Adult Education. The seminars were organised by and chaired by the co-editors of this volume, which is comprised of the papers presented.

They range widely over the territory: some attempt a definition of public value, others rest on the assumption that educational opportunity for adults is by definition a good one, and that public value ensues. The collective intention was and is to contribute to and seek to progress the necessary debate about the importance of adult learning, to explore at least in part its contribution to the general good, and perhaps to remind us all, and government ministers in particular, that the debate and the policy should be about more than skills acquisition. Hence the title.

No-one associated with this book wants to question the importance of the development of a highly-skilled workforce. This country has a long-standing problem with its levels of intermediate skills, and has higher proportions than competitor nations of people with no qualifications at all. The international comparisons are well documented and need no further rehearsal here: Chris Humphries' chapter, *Skills and the Global Economy*, does the job admirably. What concerns many observers is the impact of current Government strategies on much of the rest of adult education, and the radical restructuring of the further and adult education sector.

In 1997 the incoming Labour Government had a clear and ambitious commitment to lifelong learning. David Blunkett's much-quoted Preface to The Learning Age, 1998 – now the only part of that document that anyone remembers – was inspirational and holistic in its vision. His Remit Letter to the Learning and Skills Council in 2000 was similarly visionary:

> *'Learning has a major contribution to play in sustaining a civilised and cohesive society. . . It strengthens families, builds stronger neighbourhoods, helps older people to stay healthy and active, and encourages independence for all by opening up new opportunities – including the chance to explore art, music and literature. And what was available only to the few can, in this new millennium, be enjoyed and taken advantage of by the many.'*

The 2005 Skills White Paper puts a different emphasis on the educational objectives, with a clear shift towards the utilitarian:

> *'Skills are central to achieving our national goals of prosperity and fairness. They are an essential contributor to a successful, wealth-creating economy. They help businesses become more productive and profitable. They help individuals achieve their ambitions for themselves, their families and their communities.'*

What has changed is the relative importance that is now placed on the objectives of post-compulsory education. Ministers still seek to reassure that lifelong learning remains a key aspiration and they vehemently claim that social justice is as high a priority as economic growth, but these claims are belied by the policies and the resources that support them. Around a million learners have been lost to adult classes in the last two years, because of rising fee levels but also because of a reduced offer in many colleges and centres. There are fewer foreign language classes, fewer ICT courses, fewer students. The shift to a so-called demand-led system in practice means students are actively encouraged to learn as long as they demand what the Government and the LSC are willing to provide: literacy, numeracy, or a first 'full' Level 2 qualification. Anyone demanding anything else will be paying a good deal more. The new ideologies have shifted massive resource away from adult and community learning on to vocational provision, and towards training defined by employers. At the same time resources are also being moved away from long-standing and successful vocational qualifications, mainly part-time, that people and employers have used to acquire and up-grade work-related skills and qualifications, because they are not 'full', and therefore do not contribute to what are poorly-formulated targets.

Train to Gain, the flagship programme underpinning the policy, will cost £473 million in 2007/8. Its value and effectiveness is, to date, far from proven. It failed to reach its targets in the first year of operation and in a survey conducted by the Chartered Institute of Personnel and Development, reported in July 2007, only one in three employers with experience of Train to Gain was satisfied that it met their needs. Too many of the qualifications being gained are simply the accreditation of skills already held – in other words they add nothing to our national competitiveness – and too few employees follow through to seek qualifications. The issue of 'deadweight' – the significant proportions of training now encompassed in and paid for by the scheme that would have taken place anyway, at employer's cost – is being accepted or ignored.

Ministers can reasonably claim that it is too early to tell whether the strategies are working, but enormous weight, and resource, is being placed on the Train to Gain programme without any satisfactory evidence that it can do what is required. We need a change in the educational culture of this country: it is hard to see how it can be achieved through this mechanism. Such a scheme is certainly a necessary part of a wide range of opportunity that should be on offer to adult learners, but it should not be virtually the sole strategy, and it should not be promoted at the expense of much other valuable work. What is more, it is in itself expensive provision. Simone Delorenzi of *ippr* (*Learning for Life, ippr 2007*) has shown that this year's £473m is expected to pay for about 200,000 full Level 2 starts and about 34,500 basic skills starts, from which she calculates that each new learner will cost £2020. This buys on average 50 hours of 'contact time', of which only around a third is actual teaching. (The rest is assessment and portfolio-building.) Delorenzi argues that considerably better value for money would be gained by investing the same amount of money in full-time learning programmes, in which teaching and learning, rather than assessment and employer subsidy are the focus, and would be likely to produce better and longer-lasting results.

The present strategy appears to be set for at least three years, with the roll-out of the plans derived from the Leitch Review of Skills needs requiring further 're-balancing' of budgets (i.e. more money into the identified priority areas at the expense of other kinds of adult provision.)

One thing that will need to be addressed, however, is the demonstrable inadequacies of the qualifications structures on which the strategy relies. As Alan Wells, former Director of the Basic Skills Agency, pointed out in an article in The Guardian in September 2007, some qualifications are more equal than others. The benchmark of Level 2 qualifications is five 'good' GCSEs: five passes at A-C grade. That is what the large majority of young people should be achieving at age 16, after five years of secondary education. It's a good target, and a good platform for progression to Level 3. But as Wells points out, there has to be considerable doubt as to whether all Level 2 qualifications are of equivalent value. He cites the new Personal Licence required by those working in the hospitality industries in order that they can supervise the sale of alcohol. Apparently this Licence can be obtained after a one-day course, followed by a 40 question multiple-choice exam. The pass rate is about 95%, and it is a Level 2 qualification. One assumes – indeed hopes – that it is not a 'full-fat' L2, but it will still carry the badge.

This is far from being the only problem with the Level 2 strategy. The pursuit of the targets imposed and the consequent direction of funding has had the effect of reducing or eliminating a whole range of provision for people at lower levels, Entry and Level 1, thus removing some of the lower rungs on the ladder. It insists on funding only the so-called 'full-fat' Level 2, when often people need only to top-up in order to reach Level 2. It funds only a first Level 2: if a learner has an old, out-of-date or redundant qualification and needs to change direction with a new one, he or she is not eligible. GCSEs undertaken years ago may have no relevance to a chosen career, but that is the first Level 2. There are, doubtless, ways around some of these obstacles with the help of a sympathetic college or other provider, but it would do much for the system and, more importantly for learners, were it to be more coherent and rational.

It is useful to look back at what has happened in recent months. Since Mr Blair departed and Mr Brown took over there may (or may not) be a change in the relationship with the United States, and over the involvement in Iraq, but the changes in the structures of educational policy-making show reinforcement rather than any weakening of resolve on skills. The key factors which could impinge on adult learning can be summarised as follows:

- The two new departments which have emerged from the old DfES can be seen as largely pre- and post-19. The Department for Innovation, Universi-

ties and Skills will be more focused on adults, but although the Secretary
of State has recognised the intrinsic value of learning, he has not so far
redirected any of the resource in directions which many of us think should
follow.

- It's a long game. Many of the proposed changes will take years to implement
  – for example the switching of responsibilities and resources from LSC to
  local authorities. It will be several years before any benefits, if any, are seen.
- The Comprehensive Spending Review announcements in October (2007)
  made very clear that there will be little or no new money. The fact that Public Sector Agreements are to be cut from 110 to fewer than 30 is probably
  something to be welcomed, but there will be no positive effect on the provision of adult learning, unless the relevant targets are redefined in order to
  facilitate greater responsiveness to local and regional issues, and in particular
  to areas where social and economic deprivation is still very high.
- The Treasury report on sub-national development proposes more local and
  regional control of public services, which could theoretically benefit adult
  learning. . . but only if there were more money. See above.
- The Leitch Implementation Plan is bad news for adult learning. Yet higher
  proportions of the limited funds will be spent on basic skills and Level 2:
  most money is directed through Train to Gain and the new Skills Accounts;
  planning for post-19 provision (outside HE) is all in the skills envelope; there
  are to be new Employment and Skills Boards. This is all part of the
  employer-led strategy, rather than being employee or individual focused.
- Adult learning budgets will become a major battleground. All of the
  following will be in there fighting: Regional Development Agencies, a
  weakened LSC, the resurgent local authorities, the new UK Commission on
  Skills and Employment and, in Greater London, the Mayor. Adult learning
  other than the skills-based will not be high on the agenda of most of these
  (though London might develop some variant approaches and will be keenly
  watched).
- The debate over financial support for students is likely to sharpen, with
  increased financial support announced for HE students from disadvantaged
  backgrounds, against further restrictions on fee support for students in FE.
  It will surely be increasingly hard to justify the wholly different approaches
  to financial support for students in HE compared to those in FE.
- The Personal and Community Development Fund, never much more than
  tokenism, does not appear in the identified responsibilities of either of the
  two new Departments that emerged from the corpse of the DfES.

In summary, although it is too early to tell, there may at some point be new
opportunities to make the case for lifelong learning within the new structures
and arrangements. But policy looks to be set in stone for the foreseeable future.

Mr Brown was always believed to be the main architect of the skills strategy, and one of the few Ministers who remained in the same job through all the reshuffles was Bill Rammell, unswerving in his support for and defence of it, despite all cries of anguish.

Another Minister, David Lammy (Minister for Skills) was quoted recently as stating that 'more adults than ever (80 per cent) are in learning. It is very encouraging to see that many adults across the country are investing in themselves and are seeking career progression'. This was a comment upon a survey for DIUS, published by the LSC and conducted by ICM in March 2007 in which the actual figures appeared somewhat different. On the basis of this, it was revealed that the keenest learners are in London (31 per cent of Londoners involved in some form of education or training) and the South-East (28 per cent.) The figure for Yorkshire was 15 per cent. In the East Midlands, 14 per cent of adults were investing in training. The survey concluded that 'a significant proportion of people in England (48 per cent) are not aware of the direct financial return on investment which learning can offer – even though investing in an *academic* (my italics) Level 2 or Level 3 qualification can provide an annual return on investment of up to 12–15 per cent. This apparent lack of awareness was apparent across the regions'.

The Lammy figure can only be an aggregate of everything, of any kind, that adults might be doing that might be described as learning. Going to the library? Using the internet? Watching 'Who wants to be a Millionaire?'? It will certainly include all who are on training schemes, whether voluntarily or not, including things like health and safety training. It really does not mean anything of statistical or comparative value. A more authoritative and believable figure can be found in a Government document from March 2007 entitled Education and Training 2010: the UK's progress towards the Lisbon Objectives:

> 'At 21 per cent, current levels of adult participation in formal learning are high across the UK, in comparison with both EU and global averages. Traditionally this has been driven by high levels of participation in relatively low-volume part-time adult education programmes taken for leisure, civic, health and social reasons.'

All those with involvement in adult education know that the figure quoted here is much more accurate. They also know that the kind of provision described is declining steeply, and that much of the infrastructure of adult education is being lost.

So is the sense that individual learners matter, despite all the rhetoric about 'personalisation' that emanated from the former DfES. Adult learners have less choice about what they are able to study, receive less financial support, are more likely to be taught by part-time staff, especially when themselves studying part-time. There is marked disparity between adult learners in higher education compared with those in further education. A member of the House of Commons Select Committee on Education and Training (Helen Jones, Member for Warrington North) asked at one of its witness sessions why it should be that there were virtually no restrictions on what an adult student was able to study at university, subsidised by the State, when the choice was so much more limited for a similar student in an FE college? No-one attempted an answer. (There are some signs from recent announcements that there are to be restrictions on HE too, thus providing an answer but almost certainly the wrong one.)

It becomes much harder for those who have been failed by the schools system to access the kind of range of second-chance opportunities that the further education colleges were so good at providing. At a time when we need to be making it easier for those with few or no qualifications to be returning to learning, for economic as well as for reasons of social justice, we are prescribing choice and limiting many of the routes through which people returned.

There has been heavy investment in education since 1997, and further education has certainly not been excluded. The Government has made the most purposeful and concerted attempt that this country has ever seen to overturn problems and failings that have bedevilled British education for decades. There can be no argument with the determined effort that has gone into the achievement of two critical targets, to increase the number of people with good basic skills, and to increase the numbers of adults with a Level 2 qualification. These are necessary goals: there are 6.7 million people of working age with low or zero educational achievement in the country. Britain cannot be economically competitive unless it solves these problems. But the unforeseen and sometimes perverse consequences of these policies are arguably putting at serious risk other equally necessary objectives. What has happened over the provision of English for speakers of other languages is a good example. And, whatever the rhetoric, we are not making sufficient progress towards greater social justice. As the chapter in this volume derived from Nick Pearce's seminar reminds us, despite progress since 1997, levels of child poverty remain higher than those in many of our European partners, and 'inequalities in income, wealth and wellbeing remain stubbornly high. Parental social class and ethnic background still heavily influence life chances'. Against OECD averages, Britain remains a low equity country.

Since he presented to the NIACE seminar, Nick has left *ippr* and become Head of Policy at No. 10. His is a significant and positive appointment.

Because what is urgently needed now is some refinement of the policy. The over-riding targets have led to narrower provision: more attention needs to be paid to the wider picture. There is compelling evidence from the Centre for Research on the Wider Benefits of Learning at the Institute of Education about the beneficial effects on health, racial tolerance, family life, community involvement and social cohesion. Feinstein and Sabates in their chapter in this volume examine the concept of 'social productivity', 'the capacity of education to support the generation of outcomes of social value'. To state the obvious, these benefits are much less likely to accrue from an NVQ in welding, for example, than from a more rounded educational experience with higher levels of social interaction. We need programmes of general education for adults, built round the needs of the learners, recognising the problems of past educational experience and offering planned learning support.

We need to return to the concept of educational entitlement. The FEFC's Committee on Widening Participation in Further Education (the Kennedy Report) recommended in 1997 that there should be a lifetime entitlement to education up to Level 3, free for young people and those who are socially and economically deprived. It remains a great ideal, and one to which we may be slowly groping, but a very important next step could be taken by freeing up the pathways to Level 2 to a much greater degree than at present. Anyone without a Level 2 should be allowed free access to provision of their choice, up to and including Level 2, thus bringing in scope all of the valuable Entry and Level 1 stepping stones to advancement, many of which are now denied. Access should be flexible and supportive. We need to encourage the reluctant back into learning, not seek to conscript them into exclusively vocational qualifications. The longer term benefits will be greater.

Financial support for targeted groups needs to be improved. If our OECD rankings are a helpful guide, and they tell us we rate eleventh amongst OECD countries for higher level skills, eighteenth for lower level skills and twentieth for intermediate skills, is there not a case for greater incentivisation of the areas where we do least well? There needs to be a system of income-contingent loans for adults taking courses at Levels 3 and 4, on the same basis as those available to students in higher education, i.e. with the same conditions on interest and repayment. Colleges and other public sector providers need greater freedom in the use of discretionary funding and fee remissions for learner support. It may need tighter regulation and greater consistency than had developed before financial constraints removed most of the funding, but these were valuable means of supporting needy students. The new arrangements announced by John Denham in September (£35m to support 30,000 people a year in the workforce to gain new skills) are good, but an equal concern is for those people not in the workforce.

Colleges of further education are not simply training providers. This is to state the obvious, but it appears to be how they are increasingly seen by Government – part of the agencies through which policy is delivered. Any vision or sense of FE colleges forming a planned national system of educational opportunity for non-university post-compulsory education seems to recede: 'contestability' is all. Despite Foster, despite Leitch, there has been little objective appraisal of the wider role and value of colleges. Yet good colleges are at the heart of their local communities, providing services to business, to schools, to local authorities, to individuals, often to community groups. Good colleges know their customers, and they should be trusted to respond to them. They demonstrated their responsiveness to educational need in the period after Incorporation with significant growth and innovation, until the then Government took fright at the scale of growth (those who were there will remember the demand-led element) and a very small number of cases of misuse of the new freedoms, resulting in a few well-publicised scandals. There should be a return to a strategic role for the colleges, in partnership with local authorities and regional development agencies, with the ability to set long-term plans and goals, and taking responsibility for their own educational character.

We need a robust, sophisticated and *national* system of credit. We have understood for years the tremendous benefits that a credit-based system would afford us, but have failed dismally to design it. Stott and Lillis make the case powerfully in their chapter. They argue that the present qualifications system is a very blunt instrument for measuring the skills and achievements of the population, and that over time credit can provide a much more subtle and sophisticated picture of UK plc than that provided by our current qualifications. They are surely right. Individuals, providers, employers would benefit from a credit-based system, and we should spare no effort, nor spare vested interests, in introducing it. It will empower and motivate learners.

We should set an educational vision for post-compulsory education, with the learner at the heart of it, with all interested parties including educational professionals contributing to the debate and the decisions. And we should give the systems that are agreed time to work, and we should stop the endless tinkering that has been such a feature of education in this country.

With reforms along these lines, we would have a chance not only of achieving an adult education system which large and increasing numbers of the public would value, but also one which met the criterion of good value for public money. We would also be taking a major step towards a lasting change in the educational culture of this country.

References

Delorenzi, S. (2007) *Learning for Life: a New Framework for Adult Skills*, IPPR.

Fauth, R. (2007) *Public Value and Learning and Skills*, The Work Foundation. *Eight in Ten: Adult Learners in Further Education*, NIACE, 2005.

Kennedy, H. (1997) *Learning Works: Widening Participation in Further Education*, FEFC.

Contributors

Simon Beer, NIACE's Regional Development Officer for London, has worked in further and adult education since 1986. In addition to thirteen years as a middle manager in FE, he has worked for the WEA in London and in teacher education. He has run an arts for development programme in Sri Lanka, and a community radio station in West London. Recent work includes workplace learning projects with trade unions and papers on lifelong learning discourses, learning and crime and learning brokerage.

Richard Bolsin: After graduating from Queens' College, Cambridge, Richard Bolsin started his career teaching classics. He then gained wide management experience in local education authorities and in 1997 was appointed Director of Education and Leisure in Medway before becoming Director of Business Development for Agilisys, an IT and outsourcing provider. For the last four years, Richard has been the General Secretary of the Workers' Educational Association (WEA) during which time its performance and reputation have improved significantly. Richard was awarded a Harkness Fellowship at the University of Pittsburgh in 1990/1. He is a board member of the QIA, a governor of a Kent primary school and has also served as a governor in FE.

Leon Feinstein is the Director of the Centre for Research on the Wider Benefits of Learning and Professor of Education and Social Policy at the Institute of Education. He is an associate of research centres at the Universities of Bristol and Michigan, USA and has published in leading journals in economics, education and psychology. He has also written many reports for Government departments including the Department for Education and Skills, the Home Office, the Social Exclusion Unit, the Treasury and the No 10 Strategy Unit and is often contacted for views by think-tanks such as IPPR or the Social Market Foundation as well as by media organisations such as the BBC, CNN and broadsheet newspapers.

Colin Flint has spent his career in further, higher and adult education. He was a College Principal for 21 years, before serving a further four years as Associate Director for FE at NIACE. With Alan Tuckett, he wrote *Eight in Ten*, the report of the committee of enquiry into the state of adult learning in FE colleges in England (NIACE 2005). He was the British Council's first Senior

Advisor on Further Education, was a THES columnist for four years, and has served as a council or board member for the Association for Colleges, the Further Education Development Agency, the Basic Skills Agency and the University of Warwick. He is Vice-Chair of the Helena Kennedy Foundation. He was awarded the OBE in 1966

Richard Hooper has worked in local government for many years. He was Head of Lancashire Adult Learning, and Group Head for Adult Learning and Cultural Services, from which post he retired in 2007. He has served on NIACE's Policy Committee, on the National Executive of LEAFEA, and on the LSC's Safeguard Advisory Group. He is a Governor and Vice-Chair of Preston College, a director of the Duke's Theatre, Lancaster, and now works as an educational consultant.

Ursula Howard has been Director of the National Research and Development Centre for Adult Literacy and Numeracy at the Institute of Education, University of London since 2003, and before that was Director of Research at LSDA. Ursula started working in adult literacy in 1974 in a voluntary adult education centre in South London. She has since worked as teacher and manager in further, adult and community education. She has always worked on the principle that literacy, numeracy and ESOL are the heart of post-16 learning. Her research focuses on the development and use of writing as skill and means of expression. She is working on a book about learning to write, as part of informal adult learning, in C19th England.

Chris Hughes was Chief Executive of FEDA, and later of LSDA. He was a Principal at two FE colleges, and has twice been an advisor to the Education and Skills Select Committee. Chris chaired the NIACE-sponsored Committee of Enquiry into the state of adult learning in FE colleges in England. He is now Chair of the Learning and Skills Network (LSN) and of two awarding bodies, NCFE and CACDP. He is also a trustee of the National Extension College and the Helena Kennedy Foundation, and is an independent Board member of the National Policing Improvement Agency. He was awarded a CBE for services to education and training in January 2005. He was awarded his CBE in 2005.

Chris Humphries is Chief Executive of the newly-created UK Commission for Employment and Skills. He was previously Director General of City & Guilds from 2001 to 2007, and before that Director General of the British Chambers of Commerce, and Chief Executive of the TEC National Council. Chris has worked actively with Government over the last 20 years, and served as Chairman of the National Skills Task Force and as a founder member of the Learning and Skills Council. He is currently Chairman of UK Skills and led the successful bid to bring the World Skills competitions to London in 2011. Chris is Australian by birth. He has lived in London since 1974. He was awarded the CBE for services to training and enterprise in 1998.

Caroline Mager was a co-opted member of the Education Committee in Sheffield in the 1980s where she developed her passion for further education and her interest in policy development and implementation. Since the late 80s she has worked in FE research and policy in organisations including the Further Education Unit and L.S.D.A. Key areas of work have been around the development of Open College Networks and credit-based qualifications since 1989, and more latterly around public value and the FE sector. Since April 2006 Caroline has been Director for Strategic Policy at the Centre for Excellence in Leadership.

Duncan O'Leary is a Senior Researcher at Demos. His interests lie in public services, skills and work. He has been involved in Demos consultancy work with the D.E.S., The British Council, and the Central Police Training and Development Authority. He was co-author of *The Leadership Imperative: Reforming Children's Services from the ground up*, Demos (2005), *Working Progress: How to reconnect young people and organisations*, Demos (2006), *Re-imagining government: Putting people at the heart of New Zealand's public sector*, Demos (2006) and *Recruitment 2020: How Recruitment is Changing and Why it Matters*, Demos (2007)

Nick Pearce is now Head of the Policy Unit at 10 Downing Street. He was previously the director of the Institute for Public Policy Research, and earlier adviser to David Blunkett at the Home Office (2001–2003), and at the Department for Education & Employment (1999–2001). Nick studied at Manchester University and Oxford University. Nick's publications include Social Justice: Building a Fairer Britain (2005), Quiet Revolution: Progressive Government in South America (2005), Tomorrow's Citizens (1999), Wasted Youth (1998), and Piloting the University for Industry: Report of the North East Project (1998).

Dr. Ricardo Sabates completed his doctorate at the University of Wisconsin-Madison in 2002 and since has been working at the Institute of Education in the Centre for Research into the Wider benefits of Learning. Much of his research has focused on the links between education and health, education and crime and on the impact of parents' education and children's outcomes.

Tom Schuller has just taken up the post of Director of the NIACE-sponsored Inquiry into the Future of Lifelong Learning. He was previously Head of the

Centre for Educational Research and Innovation at OECD, and before that Professor of Lifelong Learning at Birkbeck College from 1999 to 2003. Other posts have been at the universities of Edinburgh, Glasgow and Warwick. He has been an advisor to governments on numerous occasions, and is author or editor of some fifteen books. the most recent of which is 'The Benefits of Learning: the Impact of Education on Health, Family Life and Social Capital', (Routledge-Falmer).

John Stone is currently Chief Executive of the Learning and Skills Network, supporting excellence in Learning and Skills through delivering quality improvement and staff development programmes through research, training and consultancy; and by supplying services directly to schools, colleges and training organisations. John is a governor at the City Lit and member of the Scottish Further Education Unit and London Higher Skills Boards. Earlier he was Principal of Ealing, Hammersmith and West London College, and also Vice-Chairman of JISC, Chair of the AoC London Region, a Board Observer at the London Development Agency and a Board member of West London Business, Regenesis and the Southall Regeneration Partnership.

Carole Stott and **Finbar Lillis** conceptualised and established Credit Works in 2004 as a new research and development consultancy which has secured important contracts from national government agencies and influenced the reform agenda in the UK.

Carole has over 20 years experience in education. She has taught in schools, further education and higher education in addition to substantial experience at Chief Executive and senior management levels in the areas of qualifications, research, curriculum development and quality assurance. Prior to establishing Credit Works, Carole was Chief Executive of the National Open College Network, where as the organisation's first CEO she led pioneering developments of new credit based qualifications and frameworks and a strategy for influencing and supporting the reform of qualifications. Carole is Chair of Governors at City Lit.

Finbar has worked in education for over 20 years, in the private, public and voluntary sectors both in the UK and abroad. After working in training and development in industry, Finbar managed multi-purpose projects with disadvantaged communities in England. He has managed and worked on national and international research projects, influencing education reform in the UK and overseas. He was instrumental in successfully introducing to Sweden a model of credit for recognising learner achievements.

Jenny Williams is NIACE's Regional Development Officer for the South East and is currently working on the Independent Commission of Inquiry into the Future for Lifelong Learning. Jenny has 10 years experience of translating lifelong learning policy into local plans and practice within Local Authority and Learning and Skills Council settings. Since joining NIACE in 2004, Jenny has supported the development of the South East's Action for Communities strategy and is currently overseeing a £1.8 million ESF project to develop learning networks in the Region in partnership with a range of stakeholders.